ENTRUSTED

PHILANTHROPIC STUDIES

Robert L. Payton and Dwight F. Burlingame

General editors

ENTRUSTED
The Moral Responsibilities of Trusteeship

David H. Smith

Indiana University Press

Bloomington and Indianapolis

The paper used in this publication meets the minimum
requirements of American National Standard for Information
Sciences—Permanence of Paper for Printed Library Materials,
ANSI Z39.48-1984.

Manufactured in the United States of America

Library of Congress Cataloging-in-Publication Data

Smith, David H., date
    Entrusted : the moral responsibilities of trusteeship / David H.
Smith.
       p. cm.—(Philanthropic studies)
    Includes index.
    ISBN 0-253-35331-9
    1. Trusts and trustees—United States. 2. Endowments—United
States. 3. Charitable uses, trusts, and foundations—United States.
4. Nonprofit organizations—United States. I. Title. II. Series.
HV97.A3S63 1995
361.7'632—dc20   94-37965

1 2 3 4 5 00 99 98 97 96 95

For
Alexandra
Zachary
Jacob
Who made being entrusted a joy

CONTENTS

PREFACE

FOR MORE THAN ten years I served on the board of Hospice of Bloomington, a small nonprofit organization in my hometown. During parts of that period, I invested a lot of time in the organization. Like many others, I was involved because I was committed to what hospice stood for, but I found that a very large fraction of my attention was focused on practical concerns: fund-raising, staffing, physical facilities. I tell part of the story of Hospice of Bloomington in chapter 6 of this book.

The experience of working with hospice started me thinking—not just about hospice but about the governance of nonprofit organizations in general and about the trustee mode of governance in particular. A series of questions arose: Is governance by a board the way we should organize things? What are the major duties of persons who take on a trustee's role? Can we make any generalizations about the sorts of problems that trustees face? How should trustees be related to the rest of the organization? What are the prime virtues of a trustee?

This book represents my first attempt to comment on these questions. I intend it mainly for persons I think of as reflective trustees—people who find themselves entrusted with a major responsibility and who want a conversation partner as they wonder how best to discharge it. Such a reader should not turn to the book for a recipe about how to run a meeting, recruit board members, or balance the budget. Several people more experienced than I have written helpfully about those very important issues. I want to step back from the immediate questions to offer some ideas and raise some issues that may put trusteeship into perspective. In fact, the main idea of the book is that trustees should be reflective, that the board should be a community of inquiry, more precisely, a community of interpretation.

But I admit that I have a secondary agenda, for the trustee's historically and currently important role has been little studied by moralists, philosophers, or theologians. The classic issues of political philosophy are the legitimacy and limits of state authority; more recently, professional ethics has focused attention on the responsibilities of physicians, nurses, journalists, and managers. Moral issues associated with nonprofit governance have fallen into the cracks. I will be glad if this book serves to suggest the need for academically sophisticated discussions of the moral parameters of trusteeship, studies that will go beyond and improve on this attempt.

I begin the book by explaining what I think the central moral responsibilities of a trustee are. I offer the best defense I can against what I think of as the most serious criticism of trustee power: that it is paternalistic, denying to citizens power they should exercise more directly. In chapter 2 I continue the discussion of the moral legitimacy of trusteeship, responding to two important objections to trustee governance. The first section concludes with an illustration of what we see when trustee governance is looked at using the categories I propose.

In Part II, I comment on some of the problems that confront trustees as they focus their attention on organizational vocation, identity, or mission. One kind of problem that arises as a board tries to define its purpose and chart its course with reference to other organizations is a result of vagueness and uncertainty; it is a problem of doubt. Another kind of problem involves a crisp conflict between two values that are essential to the organization's life; the board confronts a dilemma. This kind of problem, which has been called the problem of perplexity,[1] is both harder and easier to resolve than is a problem of doubt.

Finally, in the last portion of the book, I illustrate what might be said about purpose, taking higher education as my paradigm case. I also talk about the board's special relationship to the rest of the organization and the main virtues of good trustees.

In the course of this discussion, I consider a series of cases or situations in which trustees faced hard choices. These cases include problems about the tenure of a controversial theologian at the Catholic University of America and issues faced by hospital trustees at the University of Chicago Hospital and by the boards of Hospice of Bloomington and the United Way of Monroe County. I also discuss some of the problems concerning the Robert Mapplethorpe exhibit at the Corcoran Gallery of Art in Washington, D.C.

I have neither the space nor the competence to discuss any one of these issues—let alone all of them—thoroughly. Nor have I singled out these events because they seem to me to be unusually important *abuses* of trustee responsibility. To the contrary—in all of them trustees have taken their responsibilities seriously, and in some of them the trustees' actions seem to me to have been exemplary from beginning to end.

I have singled out these histories because information about them was accessible and because the study of actual practice is essential if we want to learn more about trusteeship in any detail. To learn more about the moral parameters of trusteeship, we must study some things that trustees have done. In the final section I fill in some important blanks. I specify three general duties that the board has to the organization for which it is responsible: duties of reasonable support, of standing for justice, and of subordinating institutional self-preservation to mission. I then argue that discussion of mission is inevitably a matter of ethics and morality; this fact has implications for the qualities necessary in board members. Finally, I present a quick set of implications of the argument of the book and offer some practical suggestions for trustees.

For a short book, this one has been a long time in the making, and the debts I have accumulated are unusually extensive. The first and greatest debt is to the Lilly Endowment. With the support of then Senior Vice President Robert W. Lynn I committed myself to write this book in 1988. When Craig Dykstra replaced Bob Lynn as Vice President for Religion at Lilly, he commiserated, cajoled, and awaited the product with remarkable patience. I remain grateful for that patience and to the Endowment for supporting me as I worked into new territory. Others will have to assess the wisdom of the investment.

At about the time that I began this book, I was invited to join the National Seminar on Trusteeship, a wonderful group of scholars of and consultants to trustees, convened by Richard Chait and Miriam Wood. The National Seminar provided me with an invaluable support community, especially early in the project. Later I became a member of the Indiana University Center on Philanthropy's Seminar on Governance of Nonprofit Organizations. That more classically academic group did a splendid job of pulling up my socks, and into the bargain introduced me to issues and scholars with which and with whom I hope to be involved for the rest of my professional life. Members of both seminars patiently endured and criticized early versions of part of Part I of this book, and it is much better as a result. I was particularly helped by comments by Peter Dobkin Hall offered at a meeting of the Seminar on Nonprofit Governance.

The first heavy research for the book was done in the spring of 1990. I shall always be grateful to the Indiana University Institute for Advanced Study for naming me a Fellow and providing an office hideaway, a relaxed and collegial environment, and the kind of warm and gracious support for which its director, Henry H. H. Remak, is rightly renowned. Without that help, at that time, the project would never have been completed.

My own experience as a trustee is limited, but I thought it important to try to learn from experience. To that end, I conferred with some remarkably sage trustees at various stages of the project. I began with J. Irwin Miller, who, among his other distinctions, served for years as a Fellow of the Yale Corporation; I spoke with Richard Stoner, then the president of the Indiana University Board of Trustees; thanks to the good offices of David Krueger (then director of the Center for Ethics and Corporate Policy) and Claude Smith, I consulted a distinguished group of trustees in Chicago, including Elliott Lehman, Harry Vincent, Kay Nalbach, James Brice, and William T. Kirby. After I had done considerable research and drafting on the situations with which they were involved, I conferred with Stanford Goldblatt, Peg Stice, Sandra Anderson, Lonnie D. Kliewer, and Charles Curran. All of these people were very busy; all graciously invested time; all taught me a lot and corrected some of my egregious errors. None is in any way responsible for the result.

Closer to home, my colleagues at the Poynter Center have been indefatigable. Over the course of the project, we organized various ongoing and ad hoc meetings. Participants included Byrum Carter, Alfred Diamant, Craig Dunn, Richard Fraher (on whose fine unpublished essay I am dependent), John Baker, James Wood, John Lucaites, Luke Johnson, and Robert Payton. Marion Gade flew in for a stimulating session on university trustees. Franklin Gamwell, William Sullivan, and Barry J. Seltser joined us in a small seminar in the spring of 1990 and—in effect—suggested a radical reworking of early drafts. Phillip Moots, Bruce Kimball, Kathryn Mohrman, and Elof Carlson read earlier versions of my discussion of trustees in higher education and offered suitably irreverent criticisms.

Over the past three years, early versions of almost half of the book have been read and commented on by David Boeyink, Joseph Rautenberg, Brian Schrag, and Henry Veatch. I shudder to think how many times William Meyer worked through large portions, and I will always be grateful for his empathetic candor—in this and many other projects over four years. Richard Miller participated in countless early discussions and now has read through the manuscript of the whole book, a characteristically helpful and unusually insightful act of collegial support. While I worked on this book, Judith A. Granbois directed a related endeavor, offered many ideas, pointed out my inconsistencies and irrelevancies, and corrected the most heinous faults of my prose.

A series of graduate assistants have been my closest colleagues and labored diligently to keep me on task. Early on these included Zachary Smith, Kenneth Pimple (now my associate), and William Mirola; at a very early stage of his career, Daniel Frick poured himself unstintingly into the project, reading widely, organizing meetings, and patiently listening. Most recently, Elizabeth N. Agnew has been a discerning colleague and conversation partner. But in fact the book has been completed thanks to the midwifery of Amy A. An-

PART I

Why Trustees?

1

THE MORAL CORE
OF TRUSTEESHIP

THE ROLE OF trustees in the nonprofit sector has been studied at some length in recent years.[1] Most of the extant writing adopts either a social science or a historical approach, rather than attempting to define desirable ends or goals or purposes for trusteeship.

My focus here will be on the moral aspects of trusteeship. The territory is new; I want to open a conversation by advancing hypotheses for discussion. I will begin by stating a case for trusteeship on moral grounds, and I will then try to defend it from one of the most serious moral criticisms raised against it: that it is undemocratic and paternalistic. I will conclude by specifying what I understand to be the primary moral responsibilities of trustees.

I am primarily concerned with trusteeship in *nonprofit* organizations, by which I mean organizations that observe a "nondistribution constraint" that "prohibits the distribution of residual earnings to individuals who exercise control over the firm."[2] In other words, a nonprofit organization does not have shareholders who profit from its success.

Boards of trustees are found in many other kinds of institutions. For example, public agencies such as school systems have governing boards, as do profit-making corporations. Sometimes the title "directors" is substituted for "trustees," but the different names obscure great similarity of function. The distinctions between profit and nonprofit, public and private can be greatly exaggerated. In a series of studies, Salamon and associates have clearly shown the great dependence of the nonprofit sector on public funds.[3] Further, the

problems of management of, or the role of employees in, a large
nonprofit organization may be indistinguishable from those in the
private sector. It is a great mistake to romanticize or idealize the
nonprofit world.

Thus, trusteeship is not confined to the so-called third sector—
the part of our society differentiated from government, on the one
hand, and profit-making organizations, on the other. Many of the
principles I discuss in this book may be applicable to the situation
of trustees in other kinds of institutions, but I do not claim such
generalizability. Indeed, I will argue that the *moral* duties of trustees of nonprofit institutions derive from the unique structure of
their relationships with beneficiaries and founders.

It is striking that our society has chosen to meet many social
needs through institutions in which considerable governing authority
lies with trustees. Numerous services provided by nonprofit organizations in the United States are provided by government agencies
or established churches in other countries. American history and
polity have led us to take a distinctive course. The existence of an
active and vibrant third sector signals our awareness that we have
communal obligations extending beyond the current reach of government, but it also—if indirectly—signals our unwillingness to use
the taxing power to pay for them. In fact, the lack of serious thought
about the moral authority and role of trustees reflects our ongoing
ambivalence about government and authority in general.

Trusteeship as a form of relationship arose in Roman law and has
been refined in England and America. The motives for its development have always been twofold. Positively, the arrangement serves a
desire to accomplish some purpose—protection of an individual or
property, or support for a public good (religious devotion, education, or health care) through creation of institutions such as monasteries, schools, or hospitals. Negatively, trusteeship reflects an attempt to ensure that power and property do not pass into the hands
of the state.[4] For centuries, institutions controlled by trustees have
constituted a system of tax avoidance as well as a mechanism to support private action for the public good. In fact, a significant fraction
of the legislation that controls trustees is designed to combine an

incentive to work for the public good with a mechanism for avoiding the payment of taxes.

I will argue that the responsibilities of trustees of nonprofit organizations differ from those of trustees of other organizations. I propose three principles that should guide their work—the fiduciary principle, the common good principle, and the obligation to act as a community of interpretation.

The Fiduciary Principle

Trusteeship is a special kind of moral responsibility, distinguished from some other fiduciary duties by the fact that it is triadic. In its simplest form, it comprises an entruster, a trustee, and a beneficiary. The entruster sets up the arrangement by formulating a purpose and transferring power to the trustee, who then acts on behalf of the entruster for the benefit of the beneficiary. Thus, trusteeship is not a simple two-party fiduciary relationship between two individuals: professional and client, man and woman. In its tripartite formulation, it more closely resembles the relationship between parents whose love for each other leads to a bond with their children, or a religious ethic in which duties to other persons are dependent on a prior relationship with God. The trustee's actions for the beneficiary, like those of a spouse or a disciple, are always constrained in some way by a prior relationship or person—by the will of the founder or by the purpose for which the organization was created.

I will call the idea that trustees must begin with their special relationship to person or purpose the *fiduciary principle*. The trustee form of governance is defined by loyalty to the purpose for which the organization was created. In the simplest form of trusteeship, this loyalty is personalized as identification with the particular objectives of the donor or founders. It is a conservative principle in the sense that it inevitably leads to concern with the history of the organization, which should become what Bellah and colleagues call a "community of memory."[5]

Moreover, the fiduciary principle establishes the organization's own particularity, slant, or vision. An unusual and limiting case for this principle is presented by the founding board; another arises when the founding purpose has been accomplished or clearly has lost its significance or value. In some cases the founding may involve no specification of purpose whatsoever. John D. MacArthur is said to have told the first trustees of his foundation: "I figured out how to make it. You figure out how to spend it."[6] In these situations, specification will have to come from the board, which becomes, in essence, the founder.

The pattern is clearest if we imagine an individual who wants to do something that will benefit others. In a free society, people assume the right to make more or less autonomous decisions about commitments of time, energy, and money. However, an individual's or a group's outreach is confined not only by obvious limitations of power, intelligence, and ability but also by the natural life span. Many of the causes in which persons want to invest themselves— education, health, justice, the relief of want—are not to be won in a lifetime, if ever. Indeed, some of these causes seem to be part of the ongoing needs of all peoples and societies.

Suppose that I want to do something about education or health care and that I want to have an impact that continues after I am gone. I know that I will not be around to make decisions forever, and I also know that someone must direct choices about policy and personnel if my cause is to prosper. Thus, for a long-range effect, I must designate an individual or a series of individuals to act on my behalf. Moreover, if the particularity of my vision is to be respected—if connection with my wishes is to be preserved—these individuals must have an essential fiduciary duty to my objectives. Unless I have the ability to empower a group of trustees, I will have three choices: personal, private consumption; a one-time gift to persons or individuals in need; or public control of my resources after my death.

Even though the fiduciary principle is well established in legal precedent and historical experience, it is possible to argue that individuals' power to affect society *should* end with their deaths. It is logically possible to design a society in which the hand of the past is powerless; we could confiscate all of an individual's amassed wealth or resources at the time of death. In effect, a state with that policy would be telling its citizens: "Use up what you have; pass on to your heirs whatever you can find a way to shelter; the state—on behalf of the public—reserves the right to determine the utilization of your residual wealth through normal governmental allocation processes." Notice that a society so conceived would give individuals powerful incentives for personal and family consumption. The simple pattern of trusteeship in which a specific donor empowers trustees to manage resources after his or her death, therefore, has a kind of prima facie credibility from the viewpoint of individual freedom and social utility.

This simple model of trusteeship is no abstraction. We see it in the establishment of foundations and colleges, in sponsored hospitals and charities. However, trusteeship also exists in many other complex and important forms. In some cases, the "entruster" may be a group, and its members may have no money but "only" a sense of mission, as when people band together to form a community service organization. In many self-help organizations and small nonprofits, it may be impossible to distinguish a board from founders, managers, or service providers.

What these groups have in common with the simple model is a sense of organizational dedication to providing a good to needy persons. The fact that this dedication stems from a group, or that members of the group may themselves be beneficiaries, is of secondary importance. We have an identifiable form of trusteeship whenever a cause or mission defines a group's identity so that we can speak of a duty to beneficiaries that is created and constrained by the organization's sense of purpose or the cause it exists to serve.

On these terms, members of the board of directors of a business corporation are trustees with special fiduciary duties to corporate stockholders. If we grant that they also have duties to *stakeholders* (e.g., employees, residents of the communities in which the firm operates, or consumers), the differences between their role and that of trustees in the nonprofit sector may diminish. Nevertheless, they have an additional duty to make money for investors. Thus, their form of trusteeship differs from that of my main concern.

Another contrast worth noting is that between a trustee and an elected representative. Some writers on politics suggest that a representative (a member of Congress, for example) should be thought of as a trustee in the sense that her or his duties to constituents are clearly limited by the representative's own judgments about what is in the best interest of the state. This conception reflects Edmund Burke's notion of representation, and it remains helpful, but it leaves out of account the responsibilities of elected representatives to take special cognizance of the interests—indeed, the preferences—of their constituents. Those responsibilities are better captured when we think of the representative as a (sometimes instructed) delegate. I contend that trustees must consult the needs of beneficiaries. I don't want to argue for a radical dichotomy between governmental and philanthropic relationships, but there is a difference in priority: A delegate cares for common purpose because of duties to constituents; a trustee cares for beneficiaries' needs because of commitment to the cause or the trust. Trustees are not instructed delegates of their beneficiaries.

Debate over the balance between these principles is as old as the Republic. The issue was joined and partly resolved in 1819 in the U.S. Supreme Court decision in *Dartmouth College v. Woodward*.[7] In that case, the Court dealt with a question of who should govern or control a private university. The controversy over this point was not, in itself, novel. Struggles over who should control a university date back to colonial times in America and at least to the thirteenth century in Europe. Church and state, and various factions within those entities, struggled for control over universities in medieval Europe. Distinctive ways of reconciling these conflicts were worked out at Calvin's Academy in Geneva, at Oxford and Cambridge, and in the various colonial colleges and universities before the American Revolution.

The Dartmouth dispute began in 1815 when the Federalist trustees fired John Wheelock, the president of the college. Wheelock had wanted to reform religious worship and instruction along lines supported by the Jeffersonians. When the Jeffersonians won a majority in the New Hampshire legislature in 1816, they and Governor Plumer felt they had a mandate from the people of the state. They passed legislation designed to ensure state control of the college.[8] Trustee governance, Plumer and Jefferson thought, should not be allowed to stand in the way of the common good. They meant to defend Wheelock, who they regarded as a social reformer, against a group of trustees who resisted change (in my terms, to insist on a common good or social justice principle as dominant over the fiduciary principle). Jefferson wrote:

> The idea that institutions established for the use of the nation cannot be touched nor modified, even to make them answer their end, because of rights gratuitously supposed in those employed to manage them in trust for the public, may perhaps be a salutary provision against the abuses of a monarch, but is most absurd against the nation itself.[9]

But the Federalist United States Supreme Court "decided the question of Dartmouth College's nature as a private or public corporation by looking to the private source of its original funds rather than to the public purpose for which it was established."[10]

Dartmouth College v. Woodward resolved the conflict between common good and fiduciary principles by suggesting that social space must be left for the latter. The college could not be forced to become strictly public, acting according to legislative or majority perceptions of need. The college's own perceptions and vision rightly were to have a determinative role. But the case tells us only what the college had a right to do, not what it should have done. Were the Jeffersonians right about the proper forms of religious worship in the college? Had the trustees worked out a consistent statement of the college's mission going back to its original objective as a missionary school for Indians? Boards of trustees have the right to make these choices, and they must take the responsibility for making them. It is clear that they have to think about something in addition to founding purpose.

The Common Good Principle

My analysis so far suggests that a key aspect of a trustee's role is loyalty to the cause or purpose for which the organization exists.

Actually, I have oversimplified the issue of purpose in several ways. One very important oversimplification arises from the fact that a given founder or organization may appropriately have more than one purpose. Indeed, the only way in which purpose may be unified may be by stating it in such general terms that it becomes vacuous and uncontroversial. Hidden under the platitude are multiple, sometimes conflicting purposes. My whole point is that trustees are responsible for ensuring that these issues get sorted out—and conflicts resolved—in a responsible way. A large portion of this book will be devoted to commentary on issues that arise as a board attempts to refine, interpret, and specify purposes.

First, however, it is important to address a second issue raised by the fact of differences between organizational purposes and other ends or goals cherished by the wider society: Is one purpose as good as another? What constraints are imposed on the ends for which trustees may act and on the means they may use to attain those ends?

Broadly speaking, my answer to these questions is that only just ends may be pursued and that only just means may be used in their pursuit. Entrusted organizations are nested in the larger moral matrix of their society. That matrix may be pluralistic and incomplete, but in any given society at any given time the concept of justice is not vacuous. Although we can easily find hard cases about which we disagree, we can meaningfully use words like fairness and honesty. The fiduciary principle does not exempt trustees from these ordinary moral constraints or somehow lift trustees above the basic requirements of social morality.

Trustees must deal honestly with management, professionals, and the general public; they must treat each other and all persons with respect. In particular they are constrained by a principle of universalization understood to imply nondiscrimination. Obviously, institutional choices are inevitably specific: Certain diseases will be attacked, courses taught, grants funded—but the grounds on which these decisions are made must be universalizable. Would the organization consider supporting all applicants who meet a given set of criteria in a given set of circumstances? I don't think this formal principle of justice is sufficient to specify what purposes trustees should select, but it is a necessary condition of any reasonable purpose.

Furthermore, a commitment to honesty means that it is entirely appropriate for the rationale underlying fundamental decisions about institutional policy to be a matter of public record. Sunshine laws are a legitimate constraint not only on publicly funded but also on privately endowed entrusted institutions. I do not draw the conclusion that all meetings and discussions must be open to the public: People don't have to think out loud, and neither do organizations. But openness to public review remains a legitimate requirement for institutions that exist for the public good. The public has a right to know what options were considered and what rationale guided the choices that were made.

I will call the idea that trustee action is rightly constrained by general social morality the *common good principle*. So far I have said something about the ways in which the principle constrains the means trustees may use. But it also imposes constraints on the ends they may pursue.

Inevitably, constituents or beneficiaries will want trustees to do—or to refrain from doing—something that is inconsistent with the organization's purpose. Trustees' sense of mission may conflict with beneficiaries' preferences, and the very fact of trustee power may strike beneficiaries as offensive. Trustee-governed institutions are a potentially patronizing form of benefaction. Is the idea of foundation giving, for example, "an anachronistic throwback to the lord of the manor bestowing his largess on the peasants and knowing what is good for them"?[11] Analogously, is it morally wrong for boards of colleges, hospitals, or seminaries to offer curricula, forms of care, or styles of community that were not chosen by students or patients? Must trustee governance inevitably be intolerably paternalistic? I argue that it need not be, so long as trustees attend to the goals, values, and expectations of the larger community.

I can best explain my reasoning by recalling a distinction used in the medical ethics literature between "soft" and "hard" paternalism. In soft paternalism, the paternalist does patients a favor that they *did not* choose but that he has reason to believe they *would* choose if they could (e.g., insisting on necessary but inevitably painful treatment for patients who plan and hope to continue to live). In hard paternalism, the paternalist provides care that patients actively reject (e.g., ordering blood transfusions for Jehovah's Witnesses). In soft paternalism, the paternalist acts on behalf of the patients' own values; in hard paternalism, the paternalist trumps or overrides not only the patients' expressed choices but their values. *Ceteris paribus*, soft paternalism is easier to justify.[12]

I suggest that trustee-governed institutions are not offensively paternalistic if they act on behalf of values that beneficiaries as members of society can reasonably be assumed to hold (that is, if their actions are analogous to soft paternalism). Thus, there is a limit to the extent that trustee-governed institutions may legitimately depart from the overall values of a society—whether one describes this departure as "leading" or "reactionary." Merrimon Cuninggim's description of foundations is true of all trustee-governed institutions to a degree. They exist "by the grace of the public . . . in order to serve the general welfare or some acceptable portion of it."[13] They "cannot justify their existence unless they accept as their own the virtues and values espoused by the social order of which they are a part."[14] When trustees act according to commonly held values, according to the common good, they are not acting in violation of human dignity.

One important implication of this analysis is that we cannot evaluate the degree to which trustee actions are paternalistic without taking into account the context and community in which those actions are taken. Compliance with the common good principle requires a certain degree of change and adaptation. Actions that seem inappropriately paternalistic in one community at one point in history might be consistent with the values of the same community at another point in history. As long as trustees attend to the ebb and flow of commonly held values within their community, we can say they are acting in conformity with the common good principle.

The evolution of trusteeship in American voluntary hospitals illustrates this point. Hospitals as we know them today are much younger institutions than colleges or universities. At the time of the

American Revolution, the most common form of health care institution in this country was the almshouse, supported by church or state and designed to provide shelter and minimal care for the very poor. Because colonial society viewed illness and dependency as indicators of moral failing, almshouses were seen as depositories of the most fallen and despicable. Most physicians believed disease and volition to be linked:

> Certainly, the prostitutes and alcoholics who cluttered the almshouse hospital provided living proof that God chastised sin immediately and inevitably through the body's own mechanisms; one need not await the hereafter to encounter punishment for spiritual transgression.[15]

Hospitals arose as a response to the recognition that some morally worthy citizens nevertheless found themselves in need of institutionalized health care. The preferred site for health care delivery was still the home, but for those morally deserving and respectable individuals who, for whatever reason, could not be nursed at home, the hospital emerged as an alternative to the almshouse.

The hospital had a role in the spiritual and religious—as well as in the purely medical—life of the community. Physical health and moral standing were closely coupled in the minds of philanthropists. To distinguish the hospital from the almshouse, the trustees and founders of voluntary hospitals sought to impose moral standards and moral order within the hospital walls. Only those who could provide a written testimonial to their moral standing were admitted to some hospitals.[16] In other hospitals, as Rosenberg has written, "membership in a particular church, long service to a particular family, an appropriate demeanor—all served to separate the worthy sheep from the almshouse-bound goats."[17] Once admitted, patients were subjected to stringent rules and specific moral codes. They were required to attend religious services and receive religious advisers while refraining from smoking, drinking, swearing, card playing, loud talking, "crowding around the stove," and "impertinence."[18] Trustees served as the keepers of morality, and the rules and practices they instituted reflected a belief in their moral superiority within the hospital social system.

By today's standards, the actions and policies of these trustees epitomize "hard" paternalism. The more difficult question is: How were they regarded at the time? To the extent that trustees' actions reflected a concern for and awareness of commonly held values in early nineteenth-century culture—values in which decent behavior and good health were clearly linked—those actions were within the bounds of the common good principle. I am not claiming that they never crossed this line; the emergence of Catholic, Jewish, and other denominational hospitals makes clear that what must have seemed like a general consensus was in fact a specific set of standards that was offensive to many. But all sides agreed that moral and physical well-being were linked, and trustees understood their roles in terms of a linkage between health, morality, and piety. Patients may have disagreed about what piety entailed but trustees who found it relevant acted according to values their patients would have affirmed.

Obviously, our attitudes toward the sick and our understanding of what it means to help them have changed dramatically in the last century. The practice of medicine has become increasingly specialized and scientific; the hospital has become a citadel of technology. We are a much more diverse people—and much more self-conscious about our diversity—than we were 150 years ago. Hospitals have changed as trustees have adapted to new values and expectations about health care. To operate within the bounds of the common good principle in the 1990s means something very different from complying with this principle in the 1850s.

Requirements of piety would be unthinkable today in an American hospital (but not, perhaps, in other parts of the world), and today it would not be considered objectionably paternalistic for American colleges to require students to study mathematics or for hospitals to offer only conventional Western therapies. Conversely, it would be intolerable for a college to forbid the study of mathematics or for a hospital to offer only nonscientific treatment, no matter how much those practices might reflect the deeply held beliefs of founders, sponsors, or board. Should a hospital or college adopt such a course, we could rightly say, "You have no business imposing your ideals on us."

Thus, trustees should be constrained not only by the organization's donor or purpose but by the society in which they live. They must make their arguments over contested terrain within the moral community of citizens, appealing to considerations and values that the larger community finds plausible. Entrusted institutions should expect to meet indifference and opposition, for value disagreement and inertia constitute part of their reason for being. They do not have to settle hard questions by plebiscite. The expectation of controversy should not, however, give them a blank check. There is such a thing as immoral organizational purpose, and trustees cannot escape responsibility for judgments about the legitimacy of the ends they serve.

Trustee discretion is constrained by reasonable moral perceptions about what people need within the society; this constraint is necessary to redeem trustee governance from the charge of paternalism. My idea is that trustee governance is respectful of human dignity (i.e., is nonpaternalistic) so long as trustees act on the basis of generally plausible reasons and perceptions of need. Trustees can and must take controversial stands, but they are not at liberty to set public policy on the basis of a rationale that the larger community cannot comprehend.

Obviously, this sense of the "common good" is an extremely vague concept, one that I will attempt to flesh out in this book. It will become clear that specification of plausible or reasonable purposes is a difficult task.

Equally obviously, the fact that a board has this kind of constraint is not innocuous. The common good principle, at a minimum, means trustees must be willing to ask (a) if the organization's purpose is morally worthy; (b) if the organization is using morally worthy means; and (c) if the organization is actually able to accomplish its moral purpose. If the answers to any of these questions is negative, the trustees should ensure that action is taken. At the extreme, they should vote to dissolve the organization or resign.

The Community of Interpretation

Although both the common good principle and the fiduciary principle can have radical implications for the organization, they may push in opposite directions. Taken by itself, the fiduciary principle can exclude attention to new problems or action on the basis of improved perceptions of the good. Standing alone, the common good principle waters down the particularity and cutting edge of distinctive insights and points of view.

Thus, as a means of reconciling the demands of fidelity and common good, I propose a further requirement for moral trusteeship—the idea that the trustees should constitute a *community of interpretation*. A board of trustees must be able to interpret an institution's history in order to reconcile its essential distinctive vision with the overall good of society. The trustees must be able to select from the past so as to plan for the future.

Interpretation

Conflicting visions of an organization's mission can arise in a number of ways. As we have seen in the history of hospital trusteeship, the need for interpretation and reconciliation of the fiduciary principle and the common good principle may arise when the values in the organization's community change. In this sense, interpretation serves an adaptive role, bringing the interests and concerns of the founders in line with contemporary values and new understandings of the common good. Alternatively, the need for interpretation may arise from conflicting values embedded in the organization's founding purposes. Some organizations begin with missions and ideals that are inherently at cross-purposes, and trustees of these organizations find themselves constantly faced with the need to bring order out of chaos, to affirm diverse objectives, and to reconcile, interpret, and establish priorities as they shape the organization's mission.

The challenge of interpretation is a standard problem in scriptural religions and law. As in those contexts, the need for interpretation can be denied in either of two ways. One approach is literalism: a strict adherence to the donor's or founder's specific statements, exactly preserving the specific goals and procedures that were put in place at the time of establishment. This strategy simply denies the need to select and interpret. A board that makes this mistake ignores the fact that time changes human needs and human society—a fact that provides part of the rationale for the very existence of a board of trustees. A trustee cannot simply be an animated tool but must be free to judge which actions cohere with the aims of the founders. If those judgments were unnecessary, there would be no need for the trustee.

The polar error from literalism we might call modernism. In a religious context, modernism means ignoring any particularity of the founding documents that is not rationally justifiable in the present. Trustees make this mistake if they forget the specificity of the donor or the purpose for which the organization was created. Modernism is a kind of institutional amnesia, and it is wrong in principle because it betrays the fiduciary constraint that is at the very core of trusteeship.

This point is clear with reference to an organization's charter, a document written in a particular time and place with certain specific problems in mind. As time passes, it retains relevance to institutional policy choices, but at some point and to some degree the specific situation visualized by the founders will no longer be exactly pertinent. The situation will become what the philosopher Josiah Royce called a "lost cause," because the exact configuration of human needs and society will have changed.[19]

At that point the organization either should cease to exist or should transform its purpose into one that both (a) is congruent with the values and vision in place at the founding, and (b) serves a legitimate social purpose. These judgment calls will always be difficult. My claim is that it is helpful to think of the process of reasoning involved as one of interpretation. Sometimes this process may require drastic change, as when the March of Dimes shifted its focus from polio to birth defects; usually the process of adjustment is more subtle. In either case, it is an essential part of the trustees' responsibility.

In many organizations, the natural result of this interpretive process is the mission statement, which at its best relates founding purpose and community need. Mission statements rightly change over time—we should be worried if they do not—and they may have to be fairly general. But a mission statement that is not vitally related to the organization's life, or one that appears wrongheaded or meaningless to the trustees, is a symptom of serious pathology in the organization.

The history of umbrella organizations in America, particularly the United Way, illustrates trustees' critical role in interpreting and balancing a variety of mandates and objectives. In 1877, the Reverend S. H. Gurteen, an Episcopal priest, established the first Charity Organization Society in America in Erie, Pennsylvania. The design was based on the organizations of the same name in London.[20] As Eleanor Brilliant has pointed out, from the start, organizations of this sort have embodied two goals or ideals that have not always been easily reconciled:

> On the one hand, there was concern about insuring that the needy were provided with appropriate assistance; on the other hand, charity was not to be given indiscriminately—it was to be given sparingly, and on a scientifically determined basis, avoiding duplication of effort.[21]

The goals were to meet needs and to establish administrative credibility and efficiency.

The United Way, which is the best-known modern-day version of the umbrella organization in the United States, has at its core a commitment to certain principles and ideas that sometimes conflict and erupt in controversy. On one hand, the United Way has frequently been criticized for its tendency to reinforce the status quo. Critics have found the organization too slow to respond to new kinds of community demands or needs, and they have seen it as a hindrance to the development of new nonprofit organizations. They have argued that all the nonprofits should be allowed to stand on their own, and that individual donors should make choices according to their own conceptions of the good.

On the other hand, organizations that have participated in the community-wide funding process for several years or several decades also have charged the United Way for faltering in its support of community-wide interests and concerns. Needs remain needs even if they are not currently on the minds of citizens. Adding new organizations to the United Way fund drive can threaten the funding of some unglamorous but essential service providers. If the pie remains the same size but is divided among more people, everybody gets less.

Thus, the trustees or board of a local United Way find themselves confronted by a distinctive set of challenges: They are pushed to be responsive to all—or at least many—of the community's pressing needs; they must balance competing visions of communal needs; they must negotiate power struggles among local agencies. To raise funds, they must appeal to a significant fraction of the community's membership. Yet they are responsible for providing resources to meet needs that some members of the local community may not recognize.

At the heart of the United Way is the belief that community-wide support for nonprofit organizations can be maximized as long as individuals believe their donations are being allocated fairly and rationally. The problem arises, of course, when different segments of the community find they have differing views of the outcomes a "rational" system would generate. In practice, the United Way's attempts to construct and preserve a defensible and rational system of allocations have resulted in the perception that the United Way is unresponsive to many community needs. As the United Way has responded to these issues by developing donor option plans that allow contributors to designate recipients of their funds, the idea of "rational allocations"—allocating money based on the analysis and consensus of a cross section of community members—has been compromised.

The need for trustees who can act as an interpretative community is apparent in this situation. The founding purposes of the United Way include ideals that sometimes conflict with each other; United Way trustees must constantly interpret or reinterpret the proper mission of their respective organizations. That is a difficult process, as I shall attempt to illustrate below.

Community

The fact that a board of trustees should see itself as a community of interpretation has very important implications for the life and

ethos of the board. It must be a community in which persons can
and do talk seriously with each other about organizational purpose.
The boardroom should be the place where past and future, particularity and the common good, are reconciled. The board's major role
is reflective: Its major moral responsibility is to establish the identity
or vocation of the organization.

Thus, a good board will be prepared to do much more than un-
dertake fund-raising or assume responsibility for public relations. I
do not mean to suggest that these practical matters are trivial or
that organizations can or should be oblivious to them. The relevance of the power to raise or give money may always be important
as an asset in a board member. I simply assume the importance of
the legal responsibilities of trustees, and my own experience is primarily with organizations in which the "trustee" must do the clean-
ing, type the correspondence, and raise the money.

My point is that thinking of the trustee's role primarily in economic terms, or as cheap labor, leaves out the very heart of the distinctive contribution that trustees can make. These conceptions are
inadequate characterizations of what trusteeship is about. The board
must become a reflective community of interpretation.

Indeed, as custodians of mission, trustees may well find themselves dealing with economic issues of a larger scope than those that
can be resolved by writing a check. Standing for a truly unpopular
mission will result in loss of financial support. Many nonprofit boards
find themselves dealing with a hard question: Should we stand for
our principles, or compromise and survive to fight another day? In
the abstract, this question may be an easy one: The fiduciary principle can never be betrayed. But in the real world the issues are complex; the art lies in discerning the difference between a faithful compromise and a sellout. I do not have a recipe for resolving these
problems; I will try to illustrate some ways of handling them in the
rest of the book. For now, my main contention is that engagement
with this interpretative problem should be the core of a trustee's
concern.

People often disagree about interpretation, and many of us find
these disagreements hard to live with. The issues seem intractable

or amorphous; resolving them takes time; we often find ourselves convinced that an alternative interpretation has no credibility whatsoever. It is natural for groups of persons to respond to this situation by avoiding discussion of mission, dodging fundamental questions of purpose, or delegating resolution of these troublesome issues.

These strategies are not necessarily and always wrong; anyone who (like the author) has a low tolerance for interminable discussion and endless meetings will sympathize. But if a group of people is to call itself a board, it *must* be prepared to take the time to engage in the discussion that is an inseparable part of this interpretative task. That is what it means to *be* a board.

In many organizations, the nominal or putative board may be distinguished from the "real" board, which may be an executive committee or some other group of players whose power is not publicly acknowledged. Those arrangements usually reflect problems with both the real and the nominal board. The gulf between them is symptomatic of an organizational pathology. The core of that pathology is failure to realize that if it is to play its fundamental role in organizational self-definition, the board must be a *community*. It must have developed the habit of and procedures for talking together about issues of institutional mission and purpose. A board too large or too small to play this role is in trouble, as is one whose members are chosen in ways that guarantee they will be unable to work together. A desirable board culture will have a tradition of open discussion of the most fundamental issues. Optimal board leadership will ensure that this discussion is friendly and candid, and that it comes to closure in a reasonable period of time.

Procedural Issues

An important set of problems confronts a board of trustees as it develops its own distinctive identity and mode of work.[22] One of these problems concerns relationships with the community outside the organization. Some of the best literature on trusteeship calls special attention to the role of the trustees as ambassadors or "boundary spanners"[23] between the organization and the wider society.

This function is obviously important, but if the board is simply an agent of the organization's management, it has been disfranchised as a community of interpretation. Among other consequences, this disfranchisement will greatly weaken the board as it tries to perform necessary boundary-spanning functions.

At any rate, trustees must set foreign policy. Any organization must deal with other organizations: groups to which it makes referrals, groups that help it raise money, groups that determine public policies that affect it. These relationships inevitably bear on the trustees' interpretative function because they are important elements of the world in which the entrusted organization must live and work. A second category of trustee relationship has to do with the rest of the organization. In particular, trustees must have a good and supportive relationship with the chief executive officer of the organization they govern. There is much truth in the old saw that choosing the CEO is the most important thing that trustees do, but it should not be all they do. Further, the kind of support the CEO most needs from them is the support of persons willing to identify with the organization, to monitor its mission, and to assess the needs it claims to be meeting. In some contexts, it may be important to maintain a sense of community between board and staff by retaining some "inside directors" (i.e., staff members) on the board.

The crucial balance to be struck in these situations concerns perspective and imagination. On the one hand, preservation of trustees' autonomous perspective may mean that they must maintain some distance from others within the organization (e.g., the founder, the founder's family, or the management of the religious or business organization that provides the resources on which the trustees rely). Without some level of outsider perspective, it may be impossible for the trustees to be faithful to the core intention of the donor or founding group or to the human needs they meant to address.

Trustees also must be able to distance themselves from the beneficiaries of the organization's services. If trusteeship is understood as representation, it is representation of a particular kind in which duties to people who elected or chose the trustee are qualified by a commitment to organizational purpose. I would not go as far as Hannah Pitkin, who has argued, "Accountability may be an important part of trusteeship, but accountability to the beneficiary of the trust is no part of it."[24] However, I do contend that *trusteeship* has disappeared when trustees think of themselves simply as instructed delegates of voters, management, or appointing bodies. Trustees must have more discretionary authority than some representatives, and the question of how trustees are chosen must be separated from the question of their responsibilities.

On the other hand, a crucial virtue for trustees is moral imagination, the ability sympathetically to identify with the needs of beneficiaries or the problems of management. Identification is greatly helped if the board develops a habit of listening. If a board is to reconcile institutional particularity and the common good, it must be informed: It must listen to beneficiaries and organizational staff, and to analysts of its environment. As they listen, board members should not be excessively guarded; they should allow their value commitments and uncertainties to show, for honest grappling with hard problems in good faith is most likely to engender trust and nurture a sense of community.[25]

Inevitably this discussion brings up a third issue: How should board members be chosen? Who should sit on a board? I have no stock answer to these very important questions; my instinct is to be pragmatic about selection processes, favoring those that seem likely to produce the best board members. That outcome will require very different processes for different organizations in different contexts. It is a bad mistake, I think, to begin with an abstract definition of "the right" process and then define anyone it produces as an adequate trustee. To the contrary, we should begin with the outcome we want—a trustee who will be a good member of a community of interpretation—and ask: How are we likely to get that sort of person?

On the whole, my impression is that we undervalue subject matter expertise and overvalue social standing or connections in our choices of trustees. Public credibility is an essential asset in a board member, but even a small town may have many publics, and knowledge of the industry is vital, so long as it is combined with perspective. We find too few faculty from other universities on university boards; too few physicians from other hospitals on the hospital board. We find ourselves opting for selection processes that give us no read on the caliber of contribution someone will make to board discussion.

These are little more than impressions. The main point is simple: The process used for selecting board members should be one that will produce knowledgeable persons who possess what the board needs to determine its mission—good members of a community of interpretation.

Conclusion

Fidelity to a cause, commitment to the common good, willingness to become part of a community of interpretation—these should direct the action of trustees. These ideas are not particularly novel. They amount to an attempt to distill some general principles from the history of trustee-governed institutions in American democratic society. I do not think that lack of novelty means that the principles are vapid, however. In setting the terms of discussion, they guarantee that certain items must appear on the agenda, and they rule out some options. In the remainder of the book I will explore some of the implications of looking at trusteeship in terms of these principles. I need to say more about the difficulties of specifying organizational mission, and about organizations committed to conflicting purposes; I want to discuss the relationship between the board and the rest of an organization, and the key virtues of trustees.

But before I take on those tasks, I want to respond to some objections that might be made to my argument so far and to illustrate its significance with reference to one case.

2

TWO MAJOR OBJECTIONS

I HAVE ARGUED that the special duties of trustees coalesce into the idea that they should become a community of interpretation with special responsibility for specifying the mission, identity, and vocation of a nonprofit organization. In most of the rest of this book, I will explore some implications of looking at trusteeship that way. But first I want to respond to two theoretical and political objections to my viewpoint.

One objection holds that trustees are redundant because they lack the necessary professional expertise to provide effective guidance in complicated situations. The agenda for nonprofit organizations, on these terms, should be set strictly by the professionals who staff them: doctors, professors, social workers. This argument emphasizes the fact that these professionals have a greater stake in the organization than anyone else; they are the most knowledgeable people; they should be free to run their own railroad.

The other objection takes a completely different perspective. It asserts that nonprofit organizations are in the business of serving the people, so they should be governed by the people: All social services should be offered by elected officials or their appointees. If boards of trustees are retained, they should be converted into groups that are elected or appointed by public officials.

My response to the first objection is that it rests on a generalization of expertise, underestimation of professional self-interest, and an oversimple view of the way social need can be specified. The second objection sits very loose to the history of social service provision in this country and ignores some practical advantages of preserving a plurality of centers of initiative. But let me tell the story in a little more detail.

Professionals Should Govern

While management and professionals in many organizations may take the view that their board is unhelpful and should be eliminated, those sentiments have been articulated most clearly with reference to two types of organization: hospitals and universities.

Hospitals and Doctors

The role of the hospital trustee has changed substantially over the past two centuries as the powers of medicine and the role of hospitals in society have changed. Relationships between physicians and trustees have always been ambivalent; historically, much of the ambivalence related to medical education. Physicians have wanted to show patients to students, or to see patients to learn from them. In the last century, lucky young physicians who could afford it would spend a year or two observing or practicing (I use the word advisedly) in a hospital.[1] They tended to see the hospital as a place for learning and as a place for developing a deeper knowledge of human disease and medical treatment. Trustees, in contrast, were committed to patient care and cure. They "objected repeatedly to an excessive amount of student contact with patients," both for the sake of patients and to protect the hospital's reputation against the "age-old fear of therapeutic experimentation, the conviction that charity patients would pay with their bodies for the care they received."[2]

As really effective medical treatment developed after the Civil War, trustees lost power. With the development of X-rays, antisepsis, anesthesia, and surgery, technology could offer real benefits, and it was convenient for those resources to be concentrated in the hospital. Ongoing controversies surrounded issues such as trustees' power to admit patients, the performance of autopsies (essential medically but objectionable to many trustees), and the care of persons suffering from alcoholism or venereal disease. Strictly medical criteria eventually displaced trustee prerogatives as criteria for decisions in these matters.[3]

At the same time, of course, hospitals were growing in size and importance, their services were expanding, and administration was becoming more complex, with the result that trustees became increasingly dependent on the superintendent. Throughout most of the nineteenth century, the main qualification for a hospital superintendent was "good character"; as recently as World War I, no special training programs existed for hospital administrators. Professionalization of hospital administration unquestionably has been beneficial, but it has resulted in the displacement of trustee authority—once so "intrusive" and "paternalistic," in Charles Rosenberg's words—by the authority of health care professionals, and the trustees have of necessity surrendered complex administrative matters to a skilled, trained staff.

In this situation, trustees may have concluded that their role is simply to raise the necessary money and then to leave the decision making to management. Against this tendency I want to argue that a lay board of trustees is as necessary in today's health care environment as it ever was; only the reasons have changed. Today we need lay boards of trustees because of the indeterminate and contested nature of health care needs.

The need of a child with pneumonia for an antibiotic, or of an accident victim for emergency treatment, may not be in dispute. However, we can quickly move into more contested territory: cosmetic surgery, organ transplants, cardiac catheterization. Who is to decide if a given hospital will provide these services, or CAT scans, or MRIs, or neurosurgery? Debate over provision of services requires something that looks remarkably like a lay board. The general point is simple: The trustees of a hospital have a responsibility to interpret purpose and need, establish mission, and establish a vocation or identity for the institution.

Some people disagree with this assertion, claiming that the most important allocation decisions will be made by the choices of individual physicians and patients. Physicians' decisions at the bedside will set priorities and de facto will make the only allocation decisions for which anyone must take responsibility. All hope of identifying a limited and specific role for a particular hospital is surrendered.

This view resists systemic constraints and affirms the great value we place on individual life and decision. It celebrates the physician-patient relationship, which becomes the only relationship of moral relevance. On these terms, no one outside that relationship has legitimate power to limit resource use. This system has served us well in many ways, and I am among those who want to preserve as much of it as possible, but it has always been and remains very expensive. The cost-containment efforts of the past twenty-five years reveal its inadequacy as a system of resource allocation. We cannot afford either the endless increase in the proportion of GNP devoted to health care or the radically uneven allocations of resources that we have experienced. Precisely because of our technical achievements, the present system is no longer adequate.

Some have argued that the problem is not that physicians are making health care decisions per se, but that they are not making them in a coordinated way at the institutional level. These observers have argued that hospital boards comprising physicians would be most likely to make careful, responsible, defensible health care allocation decisions. It is natural to consider this alternative. Physicians have the knowledge and skill to provide many of the health care goods that people want, and they know when and how these goods may be helpful. Many physicians are dedicated and idealistic; as a group, they are no more concerned with gain or personal status than the rest of us. It would be absurd to try to take them out of the priority-setting process. Moreover, if physicians were clearly responsible for governance, they could be held accountable for decisions and mistakes.

I do not find these arguments persuasive. Physicians should not control the board. To start with, they have inevitable conflicts of interest. It would be asking a great deal to expect a cardiologist to vote against an improvement in a hospital's cardiac care unit. Assessing the priority of a form of care to which one has dedicated one's professional life amounts to judging in one's own cause. I do not say that it is impossible to transcend this professional bias, but, given the problem, it is important to have concerned but neutral arbiters.

Further, physicians' technical medical training does not necessarily confer moral and political insight or business skills. Generalizing from medical experience and skill to moral, political, and economic wisdom is a risky proposition. Willard Gaylin, president of the Hastings Center, made this point eloquently in a speech several years ago. He noted that the hard choices now facing health care—whom to treat, for how long, and in what ways—are no longer really medical decisions. Medical expertise cannot determine the relative importance of a well-baby clinic or a cardiac catheterization unit; it cannot decide whether myopia is such a serious medical problem that public monies should underwrite its correction. Because these issues require expertise in ethics and values, they are not simply the territory of medical or administrative experts but must be taken up by the group responsible for determining the hospital's identity. A diverse board of trustees is the right group to debate them.[4]

I do not want to argue that responsible choice by individual boards provides a *sufficient* national strategy for dealing with issues of cost containment. Rather, issues of cost containment reinforce the case for building a hospital board that can see itself as a community of interpretation and can take on the task of defining the hospital's identity. That identity and mission should determine the hospital's planning, policies, and operations. It is obvious that physicians are not the only people who must contribute to this discussion, and very strong reasons exist for insisting that they should not control it.

Universities

We can see a parallel set of issues with reference to the governance of higher education. Faculty have no special love for trustees. Thorstein Veblen, with characteristic pungency, wrote critically about the role of clergymen and businessmen on the board, claiming that "their sole effectual function [is] to interfere with the academic management in matters that are not of the nature of business, and that lie outside their competence and outside the range of their habitual interest."[5] Boards of trustees, Veblen continued, "are an aimless survival from the days of clerical rule, when they were presumably of some effect in enforcing conformity to orthodox opinions and observances among the academic staff."[6]

Veblen's point was that the academic community is a special kind of entity, and that it should be governed only by persons with expertise in the activities distinctive to colleges or universities (by students or faculty). But this principle is not easily extended to all "special entities." Academics tend to be more enthusiastic about governance by employed professionals (i.e., faculty) in the university than they are in other settings. Civilian control of the military and outside control of hospitals seems more natural. In those cases, most academics argue that technical expertise is not sufficient to settle the question of social purpose or function, and they insist on lay control. When thinking about health care or national defense, faculty quickly see that the beneficiaries of the institution are not only those inside the institution, and that the community of people who have a stake in the institution's activities extends beyond the walls of the institution itself. By analogy, to claim that the trustee model of governance is inappropriate because outsiders cannot grasp the purpose of university life, as Veblen did, is to construe too narrowly the purposes and beneficiaries of the university.

Veblen's view presents other serious problems. He ignores the fact that students' legitimate interests may conflict with equally legitimate interests of the faculty. Riesman argues that Veblen saw students solely as apprentices, valued insofar as they aided research[7]—a view not unknown today. Much of Veblen's and his successors' stress on research is right, and we may be able to argue that student and faculty interests coincide in the long run and in the aggregate. But this coincidence of interests breaks down when we focus on an individual student, and that suggests the importance of pressure to balance faculty power.

Veblen rightly pointed to the problems of sloth, superficiality, and loss of intellectual integrity that can characterize the modern university. But as Riesman noted, a striking thing about Veblen's critique is the "insistent assumption that an autonomous faculty, free of any bureaucracy, would return to a primal state of disinterested, generous and collective pursuit of idle curiosity."[8] Veblen's image of "scholars as uncontaminated 'scientific men' who [will] naturally pursue the truth that lies at the margin of the already known, if only the conventional academic restraints could be removed,"[9] must strike any observer of the modern academy as hopelessly naive. Faculty have individual and collective interests in money, status, and academic recognition, and these interests can distract academicians from issues of genuine intellectual importance. Pure faculty governance would fail to balance power, and it presumes a view of faculty as angels that the facts do not support.

However, the most important fact to note is that communities beyond those Veblen acknowledged have a stake in the college's identity and mission. I don't mean to suggest that knowledge about intellectual matters or the academic world *disqualifies* someone from serving on a board—to the contrary.[10] I merely claim that colleges are dependent on the larger society in many ways—for students, for resources, as a destination for the college's human and intellectual products. Given the dependence of colleges on other publics, trustees have a main role in governance as a matter of right.

Thus, I think it is clear that a board can contribute something essential to governance, complementary to the work of professionals in the organization. Some form of broader communal input is necessary, but that is no argument for an autocratic board.

Shared governance—in which trustees and CEO work cooperatively with employees and publics—is optimal in all forms of organization, for two reasons. The first arises from the fact that the board of a nonprofit organization is a governance community nested in a larger organizational structure. For example, universities have what Amy Gutmann has called "associational purposes" that are "advanced by faculty and student participation."[11] Speaking of students and faculty, she writes that joint participation in governance "tends to create mutual, and mutually recognized, commitments to scholarly standards."[12] The same point can be made with reference to trustees and other organizations. When they share authority, trustees strengthen their organization as a community

and allow it to develop a genuine organizational culture. They empower other constituencies to think and speak as enfranchised citizens of the organization. Moreover, they capitalize on the expertise
in their own community, thus making themselves into a better interpretative community without relinquishing ultimate responsibility. The sharing is an important end in itself, and the process
strengthens both the organization and the board.

A second argument for shared governance in large organizations
with professional staffs arises from the peculiar nature of those organizations. The issue is very clear in universities. In higher education, two styles of authority run at cross-purposes. On the one hand
is the *formal* authority of office or role possessed by chairs, deans,
presidents, and the board; on the other hand is the *functional*
authority that arises from the faculty expertise that the university
cherishes. Thus:

> The basic problem of academic authority relations is this funda-
> mental conflict between those who value formal authority and
> those who legitimize compliance on functional grounds. It is not
> possible to operate a complex organization without a substantial
> degree of formal authority. Yet, it would destroy the intellectual
> vitality of an educational organization to smother the functional
> authority of those who perform its most valued functions—teach-
> ing, research and service.[13]

A college's goals are diverse and ambiguous; power within it is
diffuse and collegial; its faculty highly value work autonomy; and
the role of economic reward structures is marginal. Efficient and
well-intentioned as they may be, administrators cannot simply "issue orders or demand conformity."[14] This situation offers potential
for disaster and misunderstanding. We could make much the same
point about hospitals.

In practical terms, it would be foolish to constitute a board that
lacks credibility in the eyes of the faculty or parallel professional
group. Moreover, board credibility will be greatly enhanced by
adoption of a listening attitude in which the experience and expertise of professionals, staff, and the community are taken seriously.

Only collegiality will work. By identifying itself and the administration with professional constituencies, the board legitimates its authority in their eyes and, simultaneously, makes credible its judgments as fiduciary.

Thus, although trustees rightly have authority, they should share their authority, both to improve the quality of the organizational community and to make themselves credible leaders in and of it. That is not to say that they can or should give away their authority, but the community of interpretation works best when it works cooperatively, empowering others and demonstrating willingness to listen to them.

Government Should Provide Services to the Public

A very different form of objection to trusteeship arises if we stress some of the democratic considerations and arguments I have just advanced. The public as a whole is being served by nonprofits, the objection would run, so the public as a whole should decide who governs them. All governing bodies should therefore be elected, or they should be appointed by elected officials. There is no place for a privately constituted board of trustees that must take seriously a fiduciary principle that relates to specific and particular founding purposes or visions.

If this view is correct, it might follow that instead of serving as trustees, conscientious persons should work for provision of more services by the government. Would we be better off if provision of all services to meet basic needs were controlled by groups that were elected or chosen by elected officials?

Several scholars to whom I owe the greatest debts lay the groundwork for this kind of argument. They seldom develop an argument about the role of trustees; rather, they stress the importance of communal provision. For example, Michael Walzer has argued that goods relating to genuine necessities should be made available to all citizens, rather on analogy with protecting citizens from foreign invasion or criminal attack. Optional goods can be distributed through voluntary mechanisms, but goods that a community perceives to be necessary ought to be *guaranteed* to all citizens. In contrast, distribution through voluntary organizations suggests that they are optional. Applying this logic, many services now provided through the third sector should be provided by the government.

Walzer develops the argument for a public obligation to provide necessities by making use of a historical analogy. In medieval Europe, society as a whole believed that persons needed salvation; the attainment of a happy destination for a soul after death was treated as something essential to all. Therefore churches, chapels, and other houses of worship dotted the landscape, and everyone was welcome somewhere. Provision was not equal—Henry VII's chapel is a far cry from a rural mission—but no one was denied access. Our own society has a different set of perceptions about the "need" for salvation, and religious instruction is appropriately delivered through voluntary or communal mechanisms. However, we recognize the necessity of certain kinds of goods and services, such as food, shelter, clothing, and health care. With respect to health care, for example, Walzer observes that "as eternity receded in the popular consciousness, longevity moved to the fore."[15] The shift in what is perceived as a necessity has not been paralleled—at least in the United States—by a comparable public commitment to provide health care for everyone.

Walzer argues that because we perceive health care as a necessity we must provide it to all. His point could be generalized to a variety of social services ranging through legal representation—which he briefly discusses—to shelters for the homeless, provision of clothing, and soup kitchens—which he does not. The core of the insight, as I understand it, is a correlation between communal perception that something is necessary, that it is a real need, and communal obligation to provide that thing. Non-necessary social goods are to be distributed in other ways. The point of relevance for us is an attack on the hypocrisy involved when the powerful think of certain things as necessary for themselves but optional for others.

Walzer is rightly suspicious of charity or philanthropy of the sort that has often motivated nonprofit trustees, because charity breeds "arrogance" in the giver as well as "dependency, deference and passivity" in the recipient. He acknowledges that public provision through a welfare system can share these disadvantages,[16] but he contends that some needs, such as health care, are so basic that a just society must use tax money to pay for them, as we already pay for public education. But guaranteed provision is compatible with provision through nonprofits governed by privately constituted boards. Indeed, I see several advantages to that way of meeting needs. Let me explain.

First, it is not at all clear that communal provision is most effectively done through government taking over the whole enterprise. We can see part of the reason if we return to Walzer's analogy with religion. He talks about religion in the Middle Ages and its success at making salvation accessible. But in fact many religious persons in the Middle Ages and subsequently felt that the system had *not* succeeded in making real religion accessible to all. History has not shown that the most effective way to provide the communal necessity of salvation—even when it was viewed as a necessary good—is a state church. Indeed, the experience in the United States is that nonprofit provision of religion has increased the quantity (if not the quality) of religious services provided. On analogy, preservation of a pluralistic system of delivery of public services—exploiting the existing government-nonprofit partnership—may have the potential of offering *more* services than a strictly state system.

Insofar as we depend on nonprofit organizations to provide social necessities, we presume a limited role for the state; it is not the only actor for the common welfare. A more monopolistic state, jealous of its prerogatives and preoccupied with efficiency, would be unwilling to share the territory. Thus, when Henry VIII nationalized England's monasteries he acted in part out of serious concern over a loss of state power to a "private" sector—the church. When a more thoughtful policy was formulated in the Elizabethan Statute of Charitable Uses, the confrontation was muted: The state, in effect, recognized the legitimacy of other players on the social stage. The quid pro quo was that these individuals, now acting on their own rather than through the church, were required to act for the common good.[17]

Moreover, meeting needs through a public-nonprofit partnership has some advantages in a society in which the level of agreement on what really counts as a need is in flux. James Douglas has suggested a "categorical constraint" on governmental action.

> The government sector . . . is unable to allow citizens to opt out and must therefore either perpetuate the injustice of compelling citizens to contribute to a service of which they disapprove or . . . fail to produce a service needed by a deserving group. . . . In the vast majority of cases government will be doing both. . . . [18]

Thus, he suggests, "an aspect of justice—equality before the law . . . seems necessarily to lead to this injustice."[19]

We need not agree with Douglas's suggestion that injustice occurs any time that government uses my tax money in ways I do not approve to see the force of his point. If all social initiatives are not taken directly by government, the plurality of centers of responsibility allows conflicting values to be accommodated. Indeed, this formulation understates the level of diversity that public-nonprofit partnership can accommodate, for the differences among citizens concern *how much* at least as much as *whether* something is valued.[20] Perhaps all can agree that higher education is good for everyone, but there is certainly room for argument about how intense or demanding it should be, and just how much we should pay for it. Public funding inevitably imposes a ceiling on expenditures that is lower than some people think it should be.

Thus, a nonprofit sector in which trustees function is more at home in the self-consciously pluralist society of late twentieth-century America than it was in sixteenth-century England. Pluralism requires acknowledging the legitimacy of differing and competing visions of the good life and society. Nonprofit trusteeship allows individual citizens room to act on their particularized and diverse values and visions.

For example, public education must remain neutral between some competing conceptions of the good life and of justice.[21] Government supports public education, but the product may fail to live up to some people's fullest expectations. The existence of private education, most vividly of confessional religious education, allows society as a whole to acknowledge the legitimacy of a variety of educational alternatives.

Finally, there is an important psychological point to be made. The simple fact is that people will give more time, energy, assistance, and money for causes or values with which they identify and for which they have a sense of ownership. A vital third sector means that people have space to "do something about it" whether "it" is the environment, the quality of education, or access to health care. More people are working than would be the case if we stressed efficiency and had only one center of initiative. Voluntarily helping each other gives people a sense of being part of a community, something we should want to encourage. "The goal is participation in communal activities, the concrete realization of membership."[22]

Conclusion

Both of these objections—that professionals should govern or that the people should govern—get at something important. It is important for a board and an administration to listen to, work with, and in many ways be led by the professionals who make up an organization. Similarly, the needs of the public are one of the decisive factors that a board must consider; indeed, the legitimacy of a nonprofit rests on the assumption that it will contribute to meeting those needs. But neither of these objections overthrows the importance of preserving a pluralism of centers of initiative for meeting human needs. We are better off having a government-nonprofit partnership than we would be if we had only government provision of services with its admittedly increased efficiency and elimination of free riders.

Because we are better off with a vital nonprofit sector, trusteeship is essential to our polity. If all needs were met through strictly public agencies, there would be no need for the particularity represented by the fiduciary principle, nothing to balance against perceptions of the common good, and no need for the kind of community of interpretation that I claim boards of trustees should be. The very fact that some major state institutions, such as state universities, have boards of trustees symbolizes our recognition of the fact that they should have significant autonomy with reference to the general public. Trusteeship is an expression of democracy against professional dominance and an important guarantor of pluralism in a democratic society.

3

AN ILLUSTRATION
Trustees and Football

TRUSTEES' OBLIGATION TO focus on institutional mission requires them to be faithful to a core purpose, to reflect on the
needs of the society in which their organization operates, and to
become a community of interpretation. I have discussed these matters in very general terms. To illustrate, I will turn to a specific history of board action.

The Football Scandal at SMU

Southern Methodist University (SMU), located in Dallas, is a private university of just under nine thousand students. The school
is successful academically and financially, with an endowment of
$334,643,000 on June 30, 1989.[1] An institution of high distinction
in many respects, SMU nevertheless drew nationwide attention in
1987 when the National Collegiate Athletic Association (NCAA)
suspended its football team for one year because of evidence of flagrant and persistent payments to players. More scandalous than the
rule infractions themselves, however, was the fact that the chairman
of the Board of Governors (the Executive Committee of SMU's
Board of Trustees)[2] had been aware of the payments for several years
and had actively attempted to mislead both the administration and
the board with respect to the matter.

I will describe and evaluate events at SMU at a little length, but
my reason for doing so is not to excoriate SMU. As I write, several other major universities are under investigation or suspicion for
comparable actions, and we can expect these controversies to con-

tinue. SMU is of interest precisely because it is *not* unique, but a paradigm case of a perennial problem in American higher education. Indeed, once the sensational layers are pared away, the SMU story raises hard issues about which reasonable persons may well be in doubt. My account must be specific if it is to be credible, but I am interested in raising a complex of issues that is recurrent, perhaps universal.

To understand what happened at SMU, one must first understand the structure of the governance system that was in place in the mid-1980s. According to the Articles of Incorporation, the Board of Trustees at SMU comprised the Bishops of the South Central Jurisdiction of the Methodist Church ex officio and seventy-five others.[3] Because the board was so large, the members delegated actual responsibility to a twenty-one-member Executive Committee or "Board of Governors" in 1967. Each of the two boards had its own hierarchy and chair. The Board of Governors met every month, but the full Board of Trustees met only twice a year to hear the reports of the Board of Governors and those of the university's president. According to the Bishops' Committee's report of its investigation of the scandal that developed, "In practice the Trustees were not informed in any detail, and were not asked to ratify, the actions of the Board of Governors. Trustees were informed only of what was considered to be of general interest."[4]

Abuses in SMU's athletic program were substantial. Athletes received rent-free apartments, offers of cars purchased with "loans" that need never be repaid, and direct cash payments for living expenses. All of these payments directly violated NCAA rules. Indeed, the NCAA had repeatedly investigated and cited SMU for infractions, imposing sanctions in 1958, 1964, 1974, 1975, 1981, and 1985.

The 1985 sanction resulted from protracted investigations that began in 1983. Throughout that process the president and the "leadership" adopted an attitude that has been described as "adversarial" toward the NCAA.[5] The leadership was enraged because the charges against SMU originated with players SMU had recruited but who had turned down the school for greener pastures elsewhere. They were convinced that if they talked to players who had chosen SMU over competing schools, they would discover information they could use as the basis for tit-for-tat charges. Instead, to their chagrin, they discovered continuing payments to their own football players. The president and leadership knew of these payments in November 1983.[6]

During the 1983–85 investigation, William Clements, who was active in Texas politics and had chaired the Board of Governors from 1967 to 1973, agreed to resume the chair. He told President Donald Shields that he was foolish to be shocked by the payments and that he (Clements) and the chair of the trustees would manage the situation. The president was told, perhaps more than once, that he should "stay out of it" and "go run the university."[7] Clements also assured the trustees that NCAA violations would cease. But both the payments and the NCAA investigation continued.

It is unclear whether Clements really wanted to end all abuses in the program, but at a minimum he seems to have wanted to dissociate the boosters who were bankrolling the players from the athletic department by the spring of 1985. This goal proved difficult to attain. One booster told Clements, "You have a payroll to meet. Maybe you should consider adding a line item in the university budget."[8] The NCAA held hearings in April and imposed severe sanctions on SMU in May 1985.[9]

But the story was in no sense over. The situation was complicated by Clements's successful campaign for governor in 1985–86. Throughout 1985–86, the university leadership tried to keep the lid on the scandal and gradually wind down the payment program. If the athletic director or football coach were fired, if the boosters were too conspicuously disciplined, or if payments to players stopped, the offended parties might go public. Athletic director Bob Hitch and Clements agreed to continue payments to the thirteen athletes to whom commitments had already been made, whatever the president might say.[10] In August 1985, President Shields told members of the athletic department that there were to be no more violations, but when he left the room Hitch, the athletic director, reminded the audience that Clements, not the president, ran the university.[11] It is clear that from August 1985, payments continued with Clements's approval.[12]

In the fall of 1986 a player who had left the program but wanted to return to it (and the payroll) blew the whistle. Neither the trustees nor the full Board of Governors had been informed of what was going on. The NCAA reopened its investigation. Cryptic communication, such as vague references to "winding down," became the order of the day on the board.[13] The Board of Governors discussed the issue for the first time in the fall of 1985, but the practice of speaking in code continued and the governors did not learn that payments were continuing. Indeed, the Board of Governors designated Clements as their spokesman.

Whatever President Shields knew, he was ineffective. By October 1986 he was on medical leave. In a desperate attempt to extricate himself from a situation out of control, he wanted either to retire on medical grounds or to be given the power to suspend the football program for two years. The leadership would not hear of it. In the fall of 1986 the payroll was stolen, but the "donor" replaced it![14] Members of the Board of Governors insisted that *they* would take charge of the investigation.[15]

To ensure the cooperation of the athletic director and the football coach, the leadership agreed to pay off their contracts, and the athletic director seems to have agreed to take all the blame. The athletic administrators would confess the continuing payments in exchange for a promise of confidentiality from the NCAA: They would not be publicly identified as culprits. The NCAA agreed to these terms.[16] But a continuing investigation, led on the SMU side by Lonnie D. Kliever, SMU's NCAA representative, brought out more and more of the facts.

Complicity on the part of Clements and the leadership was the secret those in power were most eager to protect. In January 1987, Kliever made what seems to have been the first serious report on the situation to the full Board of Governors.[17] In many ways the investigation and disclosure were quite thorough and for a short time the compromise seemed to work, but in February the NCAA administered the "death penalty," suspending SMU football for a year.

The fact of Clements's involvement was still not disclosed; Kliever himself did not know of it, and the acting president lied.[18] But by

March 1, 1987, the Dallas media were broadcasting the fact that the athletic director had confessed support for the continuation of payments; the next day they confronted Clements with the information they had about his involvement in the scandal. He confessed, defining the fundamental issue as the need to honor the commitments that had been made to players.

At that point, the Board of Governors convened the Bishops' Committee, on whose fine report I have relied for this account. Its charge was to determine the degree of involvement of the administration and the Board of Governors.[19] That committee concluded that Clements had authorized ongoing payments in violation of NCAA rules, and that both the chairman of the Board of Trustees and the president knew the payments were continuing, realized that if payments stopped players would complain, and tolerated "business as usual" in the football program.[20] The Board of *Governors* was "naive" not to know football players were paid; its members were "content to win football games, to trust the leadership and look the other way." They were "guilty of more than neglect"; they "were able, through their passivity, to deny knowledge or direct participation in wrong-doing."[21] The Board of *Trustees* had less chance to learn the truth, but they also "accepted their subservient role. Some trustees stopped attending Board of Trustees meetings. That was the extent of their protest. That was not enough."[22]

After the fact, the Board of Governors has been abolished, and the Board of Trustees has been reduced in size. The Board of Trustees now limits the terms of its members and officers, and it has committed itself to strengthening its ties with the church. It has also clarified its relationship with a new president.[23] The Bishops' Committee recommended several other reforms, including making the Executive Committee accountable to the whole Board.

Failure to Interpret Founding Purpose and Common Good

This history is particularly useful for us because it shows trustee handling of a major and not untypical issue. Perhaps it would be more accurate to say, trustee *nonhandling* of the issue. And perhaps that failure is not atypical, either. On one level it is a clear case: I think it unlikely that anyone can read it without feeling that something went seriously, morally wrong. I will deal with some of the questions about the "means" later. My first concern has to do with the failure of this board to reflect on its founding purpose.

Let's begin by analyzing the argument that they were working toward ends that might have been justifiable. One might argue that the quality of undergraduate and graduate education at SMU never suffered and that the leadership was being strictly pragmatic. They had a problem with boosters who were out of control, and they were engaged in damage control. Moreover, NCAA policies on support for athletes were not revealed at Sinai; it is not clear that, apart from violating the regulations, the payments harmed the athletes or interfered with their education. The leadership may have seen themselves as trying to make responsible decisions, honoring commitments they had made, protecting the university from harmful scandal, and serving the interests of university beneficiaries who loved SMU football above all else. One might even go so far as to argue that the leadership permitted the payment program because they believed that providing high-quality football entertainment to the community was in effect the best way to respond to the needs and interests of SMU's "beneficiaries."[24]

I want to engage these arguments on their merits, but my primary contention is that these are precisely the kinds of issues that the board should have been discussing. Many of the problems at SMU can be traced to a common misperception about the role of a board—that to be worthwhile it must *do* something. The inference is that a good board is a managerially or entrepreneurially active board; the assumption is that when the school is in trouble the board must engage in crisis management. In fact, that is a role a college board is ill-suited to play.

Instead of doing something, the SMU trustees needed to *be* something: a community in which purposes were identified, defined, discussed, and assigned priorities. It is a limited but critically important role. Developments in the academic community that are of such magnitude that the very identity of the university is at stake are precisely those developments with which the trustees must be involved, and for which they must take responsibility—however collaboratively they may work with other constituencies. The reason is very simple: Trustees are guardians of institutional identity. If they default when identity questions are at stake, they have surrendered their most important reason for being.

The Fiduciary Principle

That said, I want to suggest the line of argument I think should have prevailed on the SMU board. My first point is that the strictly pragmatic argument, if taken seriously, amounts to an assertion of the irrelevance of what I have called the fiduciary principle and to the suggestion that trustees are unconstrained by it as they make decisions. I have argued that trustees should begin with a commitment to the purposes that inspired the organization's founding; I have also argued that they must take responsibility for interpreting the meaning of those purposes in changing circumstances. Thus, as a first step in discussing the responsibilities of SMU's trustees in the football scandals of the 1980s, it seems natural to look to SMU's founding purpose as expressed in its charter and mission statements. According to the *SMU Bulletin*:

> The mission of Southern Methodist University is to fulfill its promise as a private university of the highest quality. The university must maintain the traditional values of academic freedom and open inquiry as well as its United Methodist heritage.
>
> To fulfill its mission, the university must maintain a size of enrollment and campus that maximizes educational opportunity [and] . . . must secure and effectively manage resources of finance and environment that will support its instruction, research, and service.
>
> In instruction, the University must offer a broad range of high-quality undergraduate programs, committed to the centrality of liberal arts education. In addition to preparing students for . . . their life work, the University must enhance their social, moral, intellectual and religious development so that they may lead worthy lives as individuals and citizens of the nation and the world. . . . [25]

The text continues with paragraphs on research and service; athletics are regarded as a form of service.

This mission statement sets several different contexts in which trustees might debate policy on payment to athletes. I will proceed from the narrowest to the broadest. First, the statement affirms that SMU is a university that is to "maintain the values" of its "United Methodist heritage." Exactly what those values are and how they are to be maintained is not spelled out, but we can find a thoughtful statement of the values in *The Book of Discipline of the United Methodist Church 1984*.[26] Responsibility for the denomination's affiliations with colleges and universities falls to the Division of Higher Education within the General Board of Higher Education and Ministry. Among that division's objectives is "to help the agencies of the Church and higher education participate in the greater realization of a fully humane society committed to freedom and truth, love, justice, peace and personal integrity." Moreover, the division is

> To foster within educational institutions the highest educational standards, the soundest business practices, the finest ethical and moral principles, and especially Christian ideals; to help people experience release from enslavement, fear, and violence; and to help people live in love.[27]

Reconciling the administrative practices during the troubled times at SMU with these ideals and objectives seems difficult.

Moreover, it is worth noting that the Methodist Church had a mechanism in place for enforcement. The denomination created a University Senate to function as a "professional educational advisory agency for The United Methodist Church and all educational institutions related to it."[28] Among the functions of the University Senate is approval of claims of institutional affiliation with the Methodist Church, including renewed affiliation.[29] Thus, at a minimum, the church could have deaffiliated itself from SMU, and the bishops on the board had a set of standards to which they could appeal in arguments about the course the university ought to chart.

These arguments may not be decisive, even in a purely Methodist context, for it is unclear that religious values can be directly applied to the university. As John Deschner argued in a presentation at SMU just before the scandal broke, there is a kind of "essential indirectness" in the relation of faith and higher education in which Christianity requires "critical clarification of values for the common good" and the "teaching of humane values" but not the imposition of the doctrinal affirmations of the church.[30] Differing configurations of values are possible. But the church does stand for something, and trustees should have been asking themselves about the coherence between their religious commitments and their academic responsibilities.

At a second and somewhat broader level, however, a question of academic priorities arises. Where and how does intercollegiate athletics enter into that picture? Was it a necessity in the minds of the founders? Or in those of their successors who worked out the current mission statement? At the moment, athletics is seen in the mission statement as only one of several service functions of the university.

Of course, the founders may well have failed to anticipate many phenomena that would characterize SMU in the twentieth century—the development of professional schools, or the emergence of various topics of scientific inquiry, for example. They might have disagreed with many of the principles or beliefs cherished by scholars on the faculty, even the divinity school faculty. Change and disagreement do not in themselves indicate that SMU has departed from its founding purpose, for these are problems of a kind that founders reasonably could foresee. Founding an undergraduate college is essentially an act of beginning a community of discovery and argument, even if the founders are sure in their minds about the right conclusions of discovery and argument. To deny these possibilities would amount to a kind of literalism about the charter and its ongoing reinterpretation in mission statements. If those statements are so vague as to be irrelevant to this situation, that says a great deal about the failure of university governance in general— and the board in particular—to take their responsibility seriously.

My main point here, however, is that founding a college or university is not the same thing as founding an organization for public entertainment—be it entertainment in music, dance, or athletics. The act of founding a college cannot mean anything that the founder or ongoing trustees may want it to mean; it means identifying oneself and one's resources with a particular type of social institution, however broad the category of such institutions may be. Thus, the trustees must ask whether athletic programs of this type are compatible with continuation of a college or university as an institution of higher education, or as a college or university rightly understood.

I do not want to argue for a narrow definition of the role of a college or university, or even against high-profile competitive intercollegiate athletics. Competitive sports may well serve important educational ends, despite many abuses;[31] they have provided an entree to education for some disadvantaged persons, for example. Moreover, it is acceptable and sometimes socially desirable for an institution to perform more than one social role. A hospital may serve an educational function in addition to fulfilling its primary role as a provider of health care. On analogy, a college or university may capitalize on its human and physical resources to bring high-quality performance and polished athletic or musical skills before the public.

The issue is confusion of the essential with the optional or accidental—of displacing the essential commitment to education with a politically popular commitment to provide entertainment. Even persons of goodwill may find it hard to resist this temptation, for the university does benefit—in its strictly educational programs—from putting on a good show. But university trustees who forget the founding purpose of the educational institution commit apostasy, betraying their fundamental trust. That is the cardinal sin for a trustee.

Thus, from my perspective, reflection on founding purposes reveals two kinds of limits on trustee action. First, some constraints are associated with the specific charter and its ongoing interpretation as distilled into mission statements by the trustee community. Beyond that, generic constraints are associated with creation of an institution of a particular kind. Supposing that *no* inferences about athletic programs could plausibly be extrapolated from the SMU charter, the SMU board would still be constrained by the fact that SMU is a university: As a university, it must be committed to a certain set of purposes.

As I suggested at the outset, one could offer a benign interpretation of the events at SMU. Certainly it is possible to exaggerate the harm that was done, for good education continued there throughout the 1980s. A university like SMU is a complex social organism with pretty tightly sealed doors between its various parts. Moreover, motivations are complex, and people's intentions are often not what they seem. I have no desire to present any of the players in this drama in a bad light. But I do insist that higher education has more than technical purposes; it is committed to more than an increase of knowledge or understanding. It is essential for it to be engaged in moral education and creation of a community. I return to this issue in chapter 7.

The Common Good

SMU's "leadership" allowed clandestine payments to athletes, created a covert governing structure, and systematically misled—if it did not lie to—essential constituencies of the university such as trustees, faculty, and students. These practices are difficult if not impossible to reconcile with the generally accepted standards of honesty and justice in our society, nor do they allow the board to function as a genuine community. We have all heard the adage "The road to hell is paved with good intentions." If the leaders of SMU really believed that current NCAA rules for athletic compensation were inappropriate, the university's proper response would have been to question the rules publicly—a response that may have included courses, lectures, symposia, political action inside the NCAA, or legal action through the courts. That kind of response would have been constructive for the community and consistent with moral trusteeship.

Some may argue that the responsibility of SMU's trustees is simply to allocate the university's resources to meet the wants or needs of SMU's constituency. They may reject everything I have said about specific mission and the general contribution of higher education to the common good. From my point of view, this perspective represents a complete surrender of one aspect of trusteeship. In addition, however, a practical problem is evident, rooted in my ambiguous phrase "wants or needs of SMU's constituency." Which is it—"wants" or "needs"?

One need not be elitist or paternalistic to agree that desires and needs are two different things. One merely has to love French fries and chocolate sundaes, or to find it easier to read the sports page than serious articles in learned journals to understand the distinction in terms. There can be no doubt that the leadership acted according to the wants of many of SMU's constituencies, but did that mean that they acted to serve community needs? Given the limits of the U.S. labor force and the literacy rate in Texas, the industrial shift to high-tech manufacturing, and the changing possibilities created for individuals and society by the emergence of a global market and scientific advance, it seems clear that Texas, like other states, desperately needs the *educational* products of higher education. Can it really be argued that a winning football team is more in the public interest than a fine school? Or that what Texas, Dallas, or the Methodist Church needs is an image of duplicity on the part of one of its main private universities?

I contend that trustees must take responsibility for a vision that defines the organization's objectives if they are to comply with the common good principle. Trusteeship is not strictly populist, and trustees are not representatives, but they should hold to standards that everyone in the community understands. That is not to say that the standards should be "elitist," but they should be real standards that offer some guidance.

At SMU, the trustees defaulted; they lost sight of their role and of what the university should be about. The story is unusual because the violations were unusually flagrant, and because the university did a particularly thorough job of public confession and housecleaning. In that sense, it is exemplary. But in its doubts over objectives, and in the failure of its board to confront those doubts, SMU is paradigmatic of much of trusteeship in the United States in the late twentieth century.

PART II

Specifying Vocation amid Controversy

4

WHEN IN DOUBT
Problems of Specification

M AJOR ISSUES OF doubt and uncertainty about an organization's vocation or identity can confront a board in a number
of ways. I will concentrate on three. First, a board may find that
it has underestimated the importance of revising and updating its
purpose and that it has therefore lost touch with the larger world
in which it operates. In the extreme case, we might call this kind of
board an absentee board; it is surprised by and unprepared to handle
a tough issue of identity specification. Second, a board may be functioning well but find itself moving in a social and political environment that is rapidly changing and uncongenial. This board is in a
coping situation, struggling to keep the organization's head above
water. Finally, in a limiting case, the board of an umbrella organization finds itself trying to serve the community by serving other
organizations. Its challenge and identity take the form of reconciling several competing visions into one unified vision.

I will discuss three situations in which these problems are mani-
fest. In reality, of course, the classification oversimplifies the analysis. Virtually all boards find themselves out of touch, coping with
situations they cannot control, and perceived simply as money rais-
ers. Still, these situations highlight some actual issues confronted by
boards of trustees.

Revising and Updating Vision: The Corcoran
Gallery and the Robert Mapplethorpe Exhibit

In May 1989, the director of the Corcoran Gallery of Art in
Washington, D.C., began to struggle with a very difficult decision.

Dr. Christina Orr-Cahall was increasingly unsure about the museum's planned exhibit of photographer Robert Mapplethorpe's work, some of which was explicitly homoerotic. Just around the corner, opposition to funding for the National Endowment for the Arts was gaining momentum in Congress, and a vote on the NEA's grant-making policies was imminent. Concerned that the Mapplethorpe exhibit might add fuel to the flames, Orr-Cahall consulted with the Corcoran's curators and board as she reconsidered the timing and the appropriateness of the Mapplethorpe exhibit. After apparently changing her mind several times, Orr-Cahall decided to cancel the show.

The cancellation drew vehement criticism from the arts community. Boycotts and demonstrations lasted for months; museum memberships were canceled. The Washington Project for the Arts picked up the show, and forty-nine thousand people viewed it in three and a half weeks. The chief curator of the Corcoran, Jane Livingston, resigned, and the search for her replacement seemed hopelessly mired in controversy. Orr-Cahall made several attempts to bridge the chasm between the museum and the arts community, but to no avail. In September, when the staff of the gallery asked that Orr-Cahall step down from her position, the board voted to support her. Still, the controversy did not blow over. The Corcoran needed damage control.

Even though Orr-Cahall survived early criticism, she fell in the later rounds. In January 1991, a new president/director, David Levy, took over at the Corcoran. The board was drastically restructured; the lifetime trustees who had dominated the board were replaced with younger trustees whose service was limited to three-year terms. The board's size was reduced by about half, to twenty-seven members.

This well-publicized story became a national political lightning rod concerning public funding of the arts, and it also raised important First Amendment issues. Important as those issues are, they are secondary to my main concern—the fact that the director apparently made these decisions with little or no substantive input from the board. What should have been the main preoccupation of trustees in this situation? How did they let themselves get into this fix?

Since these events, the Corcoran board has taken exemplary actions to redefine the gallery's place in its community. My hope is to suggest steps trustees might take to avoid the painful recovery work the Corcoran has had to do. Perhaps this kind of crisis is unavoidable; certainly hindsight is 20/20, but we should try to learn from mistakes.

The first mistake seems to have been that the Corcoran's trustees were inadequately focused on their main responsibility. Instead of determining the kinds of art the museum wanted to display, the quality of art it might hope to show, and the role the gallery should play in the community, the trustees seem to have delegated this role entirely to the director. Trustees should understand that it is their job to define the museum's identity. They are responsible for specifying the types or genres of art that the museum will show, and for realistically assessing the level of quality their particular museum can hope to attain. For the Metropolitan Museum of Art or the National Gallery, for the Chicago or Boston symphonies, this level may be at the very top, but it will not be so for all museums, galleries, or orchestras. Ignoring this fact can be the source of great misery.

I think one reason these trustees found themselves in the middle of a crisis is that they had not been adequately engaged in the habit of art criticism and the related task of determining the general criteria for exhibit in the Corcoran. They should have been habituated to discussions about the kinds of art the Corcoran would show—it could not possibly show all great art—and which art within that type it was reasonable and realistic for the gallery to hope to present. The Mapplethorpe exhibit presented them with these questions: Is this art of the genre that *we* present? Is it of the best quality within that genre that *we* can hope to present? How does showing *this* art cohere with our role in *this* community? These should not have been novel questions, and the answers might not have been difficult for a board that was habituated to discussion of institutional vocation.

It is the fact of pluralism and controversy that makes it so important for the trustees of institutions in the fine arts to be willing and able to play an interpretative role. In an unimaginably pallid world in which all persons fancied the same music and art there would be no need for third-sector institutions to support the arts. But that is not the world in which we live—or would want to live. In our world, the forms of high-quality art, music, and dance are diverse and rich. Deciding which forms of expression to support calls for discernment. Thus, a primary qualification for a trustee of an arts organization is the ability to engage in knowledgeable discussion of the forms of art that the organization should support.

Because trustees specify the mission of a gallery, they must be convinced that a given exhibit or work is in fact art of high quality. They should not be allowed to get away with saying, in effect, "Well, the experts tell me it's great, but I don't see it." If a board of an arts organization functions in that way for very long, it is setting itself up for what happened at the Corcoran. If the board does not understand why a work of art has merit, it will be unwilling and unable to defend it. The naked authority of professional expertise carries only so far.

I do not want to defend parochialism or untutored ignorance, nor do I want to suggest that only professional art critics should serve on the board of an organization devoted to the arts. To the contrary, I believe that the board of an arts organization must play a leading role in the community. The arts must be a liberating force, touching and moving the human spirit and helping us to see and feel things anew. But the organization cannot move faster than the board. Persons who serve on an arts board must bring more than their checkbooks; they must be willing to take the time and trouble to understand what art is all about.

Without trustees' careful, thoughtful reflection, organizational leaders have nothing to guide them as they make difficult decisions. Without a vision or a sense of identity, trustees cannot make difficult decisions about what does and does not serve the organization's community. Trustees have no yardstick, no standards, no structure to guide their choices. Mistakes—and subsequent controversies—are inevitable.

In the case of the Corcoran, it seems that the trustees decided to take a hands-off approach to these kinds of choices. They chose to delegate decisions about the kind of art the gallery would show entirely to the professional staff, even when the director appealed to them for help. While delegating is expected—indeed, optimal—the board should not shirk its responsibility to set guidelines for the content of exhibits. To avoid making such decisions would be to abdicate responsibility for shaping and defining an institution's purpose and identity—a central duty of trustees.

Doubt about identity inevitably relates to the organization's sense of its role vis-à-vis other organizations and the wider community. Controversy about the arts and federal funding of "obscene or indecent art" is not and was not new. At least since the early 1980s, spokespersons for the conservative right had found support for their criticism of certain art forms. Jesse Helms, the senator from North Carolina who spearheaded the conservative reaction to federal funding of the arts, had been active in this debate for years. To the extent the Corcoran Gallery of Art positioned itself as one of the leading art galleries in the country, and given the fact that it was located down the street from the locus of so much controversy, the Corcoran's trustees had a duty to reflect and consider the museum's position on these issues, which were precisely the kinds of issues that should have been discussed and debated at board meetings.

It seems that the Corcoran's trustees had given little thought to the museum's role or position in the larger controversy about funding for the arts. If the resurgence of conservative criticism had not prompted such reflection, it seems reasonable to think that a decision to exhibit controversial art should have done so. Certainly the appeals of a troubled director regarding the possible cancellation of a show should have suggested the need for some discussion. Instead, the board seems to have tried to dodge the controversy, or to pretend the controversy did not affect the Corcoran.

The board failed to understand the organization's place in a larger context. It failed to see the Corcoran as an important player in a conversation about the arts, politics, and censorship. As Orr-Cahall astutely observed after the fact, "We were in the middle and we tried to get out of the middle and we should have faced the fact we were in the middle."[1] Indeed, nonprofit organizations frequently find themselves "in the middle." Such organizations cannot assume a deeply held consensus about the values that should govern their decisions. Rather, they must enthusiastically embrace the fact that they are "in the middle" and take proactive steps consistent with that role.

What might such steps have been in the Corcoran's case? Museum curators offered to run an exhibit on censorship and the arts; perhaps the offer could have been made in advance. Perhaps the board could have understood more fully how changes in its environment were eroding the museum's base—consensus about what it should be about—and could have taken steps to foster conversation, debate, and discussion between and across constituencies. The board could have sponsored forums on politics, art, and funding; it could have started a series of internal discussions with curators, directors, and teachers.

When David Levy took over at the Corcoran, he began by asking these fundamental questions. He said, "The essential question for the Corcoran is, what does this place represent in this community. How does it fit into this city of federally funded behemoths? The first thing is to pinpoint the constituency."[2] Levy has answered these questions in one way. He has sought to forge more alliances—especially with youth groups—and he has sharpened the gallery's focus on the Washington community.

I am not saying Levy's questions had to be answered his way. Instead, the trustees might have decided the Corcoran should play a more self-consciously active role in the politics of art and culture. They could have chosen from a number of paths or identities. But they did have to choose—and their choice had to reflect the reality of the world in which they lived: a world in which showing an exhibit could jeopardize their funding as well as the funding of other arts organizations.

The point is that the board needed to be discussing realistic and appropriate missions with the director long in advance of the crisis. What should they have done once the crisis erupted? If the trustees had both a sense of their appropriate role in the overall community and a set of convictions about the kinds of art they will exhibit, then they should have defended a controversial exhibit or perform-

ance despite political, economic, and social pressure. But their debate over those issues must be realistic, conducted at the level of
asking whether adopting a policy (e.g., showing homoerotic art) is
worth the risk of undermining larger objectives. Obviously, this
question could never be answered in the affirmative without a clear
sense of those larger objectives and of their value. It would not be
enough just to say, "We may have to close." Arguments for the importance of staying open must be on the table.

I hold no brief for gestures of high principle at terrible cost. Pru-
dent action that allows us to stay and fight another day is often
extremely sensible. Moreover, a given board's vision may be mistaken; it is always possible to learn from the critics. Still, when all
the caveats are entered, there comes a time when failure to run a
risk would amount to default on the trustees' fiduciary duty. We
must distinguish going out of business because one's organization
is no longer needed—an option I will discuss in a later chapter—
from apostasy from the cause. If a gallery concludes that its *primary*
aim *must* include the showing of controversial contemporary pho-
tography and Mapplethorpe is the best contemporary photographer
they can get, then the question of whether to show Mapplethorpe
is, in the current idiom, a "no brainer."

The crucial issue is the prior one: What is the organization's primary aim or mission? It is imperative that the board be clear about
that aim, and it must be specified realistically. I can imagine legitimate primary aims that would not require exhibiting Mapplethorpe
(e.g., community education in the arts, focus on work from different periods or genres, support for unrecognized artists). But one
way or another the Corcoran board had to define its primary aim
and role vis-à-vis other galleries in the area, if not nationally. My
point is that no specification of mission is risk free; at some point a
board may have to endure controversy to stand up for its principles.
A good trustee is someone willing and able to debate the question
of the gallery's primary aim. Once that issue is settled, failure to
stand up for an exhibit amounts to apostasy.

In the most general terms, the moral of the Corcoran story is
that trustees must stay in touch with the issues that confront their
organization and with the social and political climate in which the

organization lives. They must constantly reinterpret their mission in the light of those issues and realities. Sometimes the realities are very complex. We now turn to such a situation.

Coping with Uncertainty:
The University of Chicago Hospital

In May 1988, the University of Chicago Hospital (UCH) decided to withdraw from the City of Chicago's Level I Trauma Care Network. The hospital had concluded that it could no longer continue to serve as a Level I trauma center because participation in the network was generating an unbearable amount of red ink. Although it continued to provide emergency room services, UCH no longer maintained the backup staffing levels needed for qualifying as a Level I trauma center. UCH did not change the level of services it provided, but the hospital no longer committed itself to offer those services for all comers at all times.

When UCH initially announced its plans to withdraw, other hospitals in the area seemed interested in picking up the slack. The director of the Michael Reese Trauma Center (the trauma center closest to UCH) was quoted in the press as saying that his trauma unit was underutilized and would welcome more patients.[3] But this situation changed rapidly. Reese lost $400,000 in the first three months after UCH closed its trauma unit.[4] They almost pulled out in January 1989, but they toughed it out for another year, and finally closed their unit in February of 1990. The result is that now only Christ Hospital and Medical Center has a trauma center on the south side.[5]

The UCH decision received a fair degree of attention in the press.[6] The decision highlighted fundamental problems in the community's health care system, particularly with respect to the system's ability to provide care to those most in need and least able to pay. The decision was regarded as the result of a political failure, and negative reaction focused on state and county government. Although UCH was not itself criticized, it seems clear that the board faced a hard choice, confronting important and difficult questions about the hospital's identity, its place in the health care community, and its relationship to different client groups.

On one level, the decision to close the trauma center might be viewed as the inevitable response to a financial imperative—a decision about income and expenses, revenues and costs. Maintaining backup capability for highly specialized care, with surgeons and other specialists available round the clock, is expensive. Still, many hospitals have found trauma care to be a moneymaker, even in Chicago. Indeed, the record shows that UCH and other medical centers were competing to join the trauma network when it started. They thought it would provide great educational opportunities without imposing an excessive financial burden. The American College of Surgeons recommended a maximum of six centers for the whole city of Chicago. Because everyone wanted a piece of the pie, at least in the beginning, the original network consisted of ten trauma centers.

However, UCH did not count on less than full reimbursement or foresee the full implications of being linked in a network with competing hospitals. Located on Chicago's poverty-stricken south side, UCH received a higher proportion of trauma patients who were uninsured or on Medicaid than did its counterparts in other sections of the city. If all patients had been insured, or if the Medicaid reimbursement rate had been higher, UCH would have made considerable money from trauma care, and the possibility of closing the trauma unit might never have arisen. But in 1988 the state of Illinois reimbursed hospitals 61 cents per dollar for care of Medicaid patients; two-thirds of UCH's trauma patients (thirty-five per month) were either on Medicaid or uninsured. On average these patients stayed in the hospital ten days. The hospital estimated the losses it incurred in maintaining trauma network capability at $1.5 million per year.

Obviously, the financial circumstances were a factor in this case, as they should have been. But money was not the only factor. The board chose to continue to subsidize other units that also were losing money, notably the transplantation program, instead of continuing with trauma care.[7] As they cut the losses from the trauma program, they assured an active transplantation program that saved the lives of many people.[8] The board's decision was not simply to reduce the financial burdens of the institution; it was a decision about who would live and who would die—at least at UCH. The board had to set priorities within the broad category of health care, to decide which forms of care were best suited to its particular resources and mission.

Allocation decisions of this sort are complicated by several considerations. First, provision of medical care is not the hospital's only business. UCH is part of an education program, and it has research responsibilities. Second, the hospital board finds itself only one player among several concerned with health care. The board's control over the actions of those other players is limited; its choices are constrained by the fact that it is nested in a complex web of local, state, and national policies regarding health care and medical research.

The complex identity of UCH certainly made the trustees' decision challenging. The hospital's teaching role provided a strong motivation to continue to provide trauma services. As Stanford Goldblatt, then chairman of the UCH board, remarked, "[O]ur trauma services provide a very important resource for the educational function of the hospital, which is, after all, one of our most important functions. The medical and surgical residents . . . benefit tremendously from being able to see a large volume of trauma activity."[9]

In addition to these seemingly internal issues, UCH had another, even harder set of problems. It could not control other relevant players. Modern hospitals have stayed afloat through cost shifting: Money made on prosperous services in effect pays for the financial losers. Thus, if a hospital like UCH wants to subsidize care for the uninsured, it must either increase its reimbursement levels or increase the volume in its moneymaking services. UCH was more expensive than some other Chicago hospitals, but it contended that persons in need of trauma care were being driven past other "less expensive" hospitals in order to get assistance from UCH's trauma service. UCH felt it had to be "expensive" in order to pay for the trauma service. From UCH's point of view, the other hospitals, by refusing to raise their prices and assume their cost-shifting responsibilities, were defaulting on their responsibility to provide care for the indigent.

Nor were the other hospitals alone at fault. The city of Chicago offered no special subvention for indigent care. Major employers, who provide generous health insurance packages, moved from the city to the suburbs. The effect of such moves, of course, is to take money away from a city hospital's cost-shifting pool. Health care may well cost these companies less in the suburbs, where the need for cost shifting to pay for the indigent is less acute, but institutions that remain in the city—and in this case the city's medically indigent residents—pay a high price.

The interpretative task at UCH was enormously complicated by issues of diplomacy and relationships with other organizations and government bodies. UCH's difficult decision illustrates the effect of our inadequate national health policy on local allocation decisions.[10] The board's decisions were constrained and its hand forced by factors well beyond its control. The board did not set levels of Medicaid reimbursement, determine which forms of basic and applied research should be funded, or control the policy decisions of the city, major employers, or other hospitals. The board would have been better off if it had been dealing with a more rational policy on payment and research priorities, and if some mechanism existed for coordinating the responsibilities of a diverse cluster of regional hospitals.

Let me try to identify several issues about institutional mission that this situation raises. One question concerns tension between the hospital's functions of teaching and providing health care. In this particular case, it may well be that the needs of the community for trauma care dovetailed with the pedagogical values of providing that care, but this coincidence will not always obtain. One respondent on a survey in medical sociology remarked, "As a university teaching service we tend to attempt resuscitation of all patients, particularly at the beginning of the academic year."[11] The clear implication is that some patients are resuscitated for the benefit of students who need practice at the task. No preestablished harmony exists between the demands of pedagogy and the demands of patient care.

Second, the board must consider the relationship between the hospital's care-providing and teaching missions on the one hand and research on the other. Money may be very relevant to these decisions, as medical school faculties are heavily dependent on research dollars.[12] A world class teaching hospital is properly focused on research, but it should also be a locus of intense discussion about the directions and goals of research. The issue is not just whether to do research, but what to do research about. Boards like UCH's find themselves in situations in which their decisions presuppose a set of priorities. They should be proactive in discussion of those priorities for their hospital. For example, they should be open to fundamental discussion of research priorities, with a special eye on improving ways to promote health in the community that depends on them for health care. This focus may require basic research into new and unorthodox forms of therapy. The debate over the goals of medical research and practice should be carried out in the hospital, and it should begin—but not end—in the boardroom.

But these decisions about research priorities are themselves nested in even more general questions about the meaning of health and the specific role of a given hospital in contributing to health care in the community. Decisions like those made at UCH presuppose ideas about these very fundamental and general questions. One reason hospital trusteeship is so important today is our society's continuing tendency to medicalize all problems and to look to hospitals for provision of services that might more appropriately be offered by others. Against this tendency it is important for hospital boards self-consciously to distinguish the goals of health care from all the desires, wishes, or hopes that Americans bring to the health care system. "Health" can be defined and understood in extremely broad terms, as illustrated by the definition the World Health Organization adopted in 1958:

> Health is a state of complete physical, mental and social well-being and not merely the absence of disease or infirmity.[13]

A hospital committed to a definition of health as broad as that has taken on an enormous responsibility, one that goes well beyond provision of health care as it is usually understood. The goal of health care is not best understood as immortality or the indefinite postponement of death, but requires recognition that persons age and that a time comes in a life when death is the only appropriate next event. I do not know whether it is necessary or even helpful to specify a natural life span, and I do not mean to suggest that a time comes when health care (as opposed to life-prolonging technologies) should be discontinued. I simply mean that it is impossible adequately to understand the goal of health care as "death avoidance."[14]

The UCH decision about trauma care did not reflect an unnecessarily expansive definition of health, but it did reflect some hard choices about the role of this particular hospital in the city's provision of health care. I take it as an axiom that hospitals are in the health care business, but that they are not the only entities that are involved in the enterprise—nor, in the case of Chicago and many cities, is a given hospital the only game in town. Thus, when a hospital board has developed a working definition of health, it has started but not finished its task. It must go on to ask about this particular hospital's limited role in providing health care.

The trustees at UCH performed adequately on the basis of some widely held and uncontroversial views on health and the role of the hospital. Increasingly, however, hospitals will have to specify mission, and that will include specifying what they cannot or will not do. This specification will sometimes be more unpopular than the one at UCH.

The striking thing about the UCH story is that it clearly shows the importance of trustees' interest in the stability and predictability of the social and political environment in which they try to chart their organization's course. It is mistaken to think of trustees' specification of mission as an *alternative* to the formulation of clear and just policies on local, state, or national levels. UCH, like many nonprofits, found itself trying to deal with public policy incoherence and default.

It is important for trustees to make this situation plain to the wider public. Hospital trustees have an educational mission. They must help the public to recognize that in meeting social need our choice is *not* between coherent public policy and vigorous nonprofit action: The two are complementary. The fact that specification of a reasonable mission is made difficult by public default—and that people are being hurt in the process—must be a matter of public record.

Reconciling Competing Visions: The United Way

Another kind of situation poses challenges to specification of mission; it arises when the public or some other constituency really does not want the board to determine public vocation or identity. Critics either think that no problems of identity exist, or they resist the identity that the board has chosen. Nowhere is this conflict more vivid than in the case of an umbrella organization that is one step removed from actual provision of services. No one expects such an organization to provide services; its perceived role is to generate the resources that will enable others to provide services.

I want to discuss this issue with reference to the largest umbrella organization in the United States, the United Way. The events I will describe demonstrate both the importance and the remarkably vulnerable position of the United Way as a system for supporting response to a heterogeneous range of needs in the community. As a board member I will quote suggests, the problems are invisible so long as the need is noncontroversial, so long as the board is not perceived to be taking responsibility for some decisions. The umbrella works well so long as those under its shelter walk together.

The reality of the situation is that a United Way board is in the business of constantly assessing the relative importance of a set of communal needs; in my terminology, it is always acting as a community of interpretation. This function becomes visible when a member agency takes a controversial position on an issue and the United Way becomes the focus of debate. That the United Way is more than a fund-raiser then becomes obvious.

What makes the United Way so distinctive is that as it attempts to develop a specific interpretation of its mission, as it draws lines of inclusion and exclusion, it cannot do what the Corcoran or UCH could do: narrow its focus. Breadth is at the core of its fiduciary responsibility. Because a United Way board must make a comprehensive assessment of community needs, and because it sets priorities for the community as a whole, it cannot find solace in narrowing its vision of need. That strategy is available only to the United Way's constituent agencies.

A United Way board must have a broad vision of community needs. Working out this vision is a political process that will inevitably involve compromise and exclusion. Some very tough deals may have to be struck. I disagree with James Douglas when he writes that a given nonprofit's "view of a public good should not collide with an equally intense view that it is a public bad,"[15] but he is right to continue that "society must be satisfied in some way—for example, by some judicial process—that the view that it is good is a reasonable one to hold, whether or not a majority of the citizens hold it."[16]

In effect, United Way trustees find themselves performing this warranting function, even though it may not always seem to them to be a "judicial process." Given the importance of the services supported by United Way, it is fair to characterize the trustees of a United Way organization as de facto public officials who are serving a crucial public—indeed, political—role in an American community. In that respect, their role puts into the highest profile one characteristic that trusteeship always has: orientation to the common good. Trusteeship is always *public* service; however, the kinds and forms of service may be constrained and sharpened by fiduciary responsibilities. Let me illustrate.

In the late spring of 1991, United Way of Monroe County, Inc., learned that Planned Parenthood of Southern Indiana, Inc., one of its member agencies, had decided to provide abortion services to clients in its multi-county service area. United Way knew that this step would be controversial in the community as a whole, and judgments on the wisdom of Planned Parenthood's decision varied within the United Way board. Some members of the board asked Planned Parenthood to consider delaying an announcement until after United Way's fall campaign in order to avoid a possible detrimental effect on fund-raising. Planned Parenthood rejected this request and went forward with its announcement.

Planned Parenthood's decision was not arbitrary or inexplicable. For years its board had felt that Planned Parenthood should offer a full range of patient services, including abortions, for persons who otherwise would have no access. It was a principled commitment on their part, and a commitment to services that they knew would lose money. After considerable soul-searching, the board had decided to disobey the "gag rule" that forbade recipients of Title X federal funds from discussing abortion as an option with pregnant women. The result was an anticipated loss of about $350,000 of federal support. This financial squeeze intensified the pressure on Planned Parenthood to make all services self-supporting and limited the agency's room to maneuver.

Planned Parenthood's announcement, and the fact that a substantial segment of United Way's service area objected to provision of abortion services, meant the United Way trustees had to reevaluate their organization's relationship with Planned Parenthood. They considered three options: dropping Planned Parenthood as a member agency; providing unconditional support for Planned Parenthood; and continuing support for Planned Parenthood with the stipulation that no United Way dollars were to be spent to fund abortion services. The board voted (24 to 3) for the third option of conditional support.

During the 1991 fund drive, controversy over the Planned Parenthood allocation divided the community. Many Planned Parenthood supporters designated their entire United Way contribution for Planned Parenthood; some donors stipulated that no part of their contribution go to Planned Parenthood. The overall drive was successful, and—using only designated funds—United Way gave Planned Parenthood a 32 percent increase for its 1992 budget.

In its 1992 fund drive (for the 1993 budget), United Way instituted a change in its allocation procedures for reasons that were independent of the Planned Parenthood issue. Many member agencies had complained about the previous policy, in which final allocations were made only after the drive was well under way; on that schedule, they did not learn the amount of their United Way support until well into the new calendar year, which made it very difficult to establish annual budgets. Consequently, United Way changed its allocation process in 1992 to establish its commitments to member agencies *before* the fall campaign.

Although this change was a simple administrative matter on the surface, it had significant implications for the fund drive. The change meant that United Way's anticipated budget allocations would be available to prospective contributors before they made their donations. In effect, it gave contributors an allocation document to vote on.

As the budgeting process for the 1992 drive began, Planned Parenthood, still under financial pressure, reluctantly said that it must have a substantially increased allocation or it would have to withdraw from United Way and conduct an independent fund-raising campaign. This announcement presented the United Way board with a difficult choice: They must either accede to the request for more funding—with the predictable result of creating problems for the 1992 campaign and the 1993 agencies' budgets—or they must accept Planned Parenthood's decision to drop out and run its own fund-raising campaign.

Bad as the first option was, the second was worse. As one United Way board member put it, "Planned Parenthood thrives on controversy: the threats to *Roe v. Wade*, the 'gag rule,' etc. all have the effect of rallying their supporters—but United Way presupposes consensus." Moreover, the demographics of the local community pushed strongly for avoiding a public split. A significant fraction of the university community—much the largest employer in town—could be expected to shift their giving to Planned Parenthood and away from United Way. The result would be disastrous for United Way's drive.

Other, larger factors intensified the problem. The local economy, like the entire country's, was doing poorly, and the national United Way organization regularly appeared in the headlines as news stories exposed problematical management and life-style choices on the part of the national director, William Aramony. In February 1992, reports surfaced that Aramony had used United Way of America funds to rent limousines and to fly to Europe via Concorde, and that he had used his influence to secure jobs for friends and family members. Aramony resigned under pressure a few weeks after the scandal broke, but for the next several months the United Way of America struggled to repair the damage and to regain the public's trust. Local United Ways around the country expressed outrage at the mismanagement of United Way of America and tried to distance themselves from the parent organization.

At the same time, the local United Way could look back on three successful consecutive campaigns. The last fund drive had produced contributions of $1,282,320—up 4 percent over the previous year. Uncertain as to what to expect, the board formulated two budgets; one (the "stretch goal") reflected their wish list in the case of a very successful drive, and the other (the "base goal") contained their more realistic expectations. In the realistic budget, Planned Parenthood was to receive an increase from $43,500 to $50,000 (15 percent); in the wish list budget, Planned Parenthood asked for $80,000 and got an increase to $75,000 (72 percent). All of these figures were available to the public because of the new allocation process. Predictably, the controversy that ensued focused on the larger, "stretch goal" increase.

A boycott of United Way was organized by a coalition including Catholic supporters of Right to Life and various evangelical congregations in the community.[17] The evangelical groups had the highest profile, defending their views in letters to the editor of the local paper as "Christian" responses. It quickly became clear that the drive was in trouble. In fact, the campaign came in under the realistic budget (indeed, with a 1 percent decrease in gross revenue). Other Indiana United Ways fared worse. However, Planned Parenthood received a 32 percent increase, with all its support coming from *designated* funds.

In this kind of situation, defenders of the nonprofit sector like James Douglas suggest the sector has great advantages over government funding. On principle, it can support novel, partial initiatives. It can complement governmental programs. But what is it to do when confronted with radically different visions of community need?—for that is what is at stake. Planned Parenthood and its supporters see provision of abortion services as meeting a major social need; for the opposition, those services are immoral and divert attention from more pressing needs. In the extreme case they are seen as murderous.

The United Way's move to donor option was a key development in this situation and in the role of United Way boards in general. Donor option was designed to increase donations by offering contributors a choice about which agencies to support, but it greatly reduces the extent to which United Way boards can carry out a reasonable allocation function. Moreover, it puts controversial or unfashionable service providers at risk. If the allocations are known in advance, the fund drive becomes a referendum on the proposed set of allocations. Part of the board's traditional responsibility shifts to the donors.

Thus, as the board of United Way of Monroe County, Inc., debated allocations, it was, in effect, working out a platform it could take to the public for purposes of the campaign. On one level, the board faced a straightforward decision on the compatibility of a member agency's redefined mission with United Way's vision of community need. That was the "only" issue they faced in 1991. On another level, the public relations aspect of the allocations process pushed them to starve or even excommunicate a member agency because of the controversial nature of the services it provided. That issue became very acute in 1992 when the allocations for 1993 were made public before the campaign began. In this situation, United Way chose inclusion and comprehensiveness, demonstrating real political skill.

Rightly, they worked out the best compromise possible in their "conditional" allocation: They agreed to provide support for Planned Parenthood services excluding abortion. Obviously, this strategy represents support, perhaps a larger degree of support than the board admitted: An agency the size of Planned Parenthood can do internal reallocations to fund controversial services from other sources. On the other hand, it was at best guarded and partial support, much less than a ringing endorsement. If United Way opted for the pro-choice side in the abortion debate from the allocations for 1992 on,[18] their position came as close to a compromise as the politics of the controversy allowed.

As with all compromises, however, United Way could please no one. The understandable increases in requested support from Planned Parenthood made it even harder for United Way to maintain its color of neutrality. The pro-life activists were outraged; some Planned Parenthood leaders clearly felt they had been let down. Nevertheless, United Way was right to attempt a resolution and compromise. Trustees of an umbrella board must avoid civil war. To that end, they will have to make unpopular compromises.

Compromise does not mean standing for nothing. A United Way board should support controversial causes, and United Way of Monroe County, Inc., was right to continue to support Planned Parenthood. In fact, the vast majority of the other agencies supported by United Way agreed with their decision; they regarded Planned Parenthood as a crucial strand in the communal web of social services.

On the other hand, however, United Way's fiduciary commitment to breadth requires the board to assign the highest priority to realistic calculations about meeting a diverse range of needs. Thus, if it were clear that inclusion of Planned Parenthood, or some other highly controversial agency, would greatly hurt the overall drive, the United Way board might have to cut them off. In this case, the board's best guess was that the losses were less with Planned Parenthood in than out, and the resolution came as close as possible to giving Planned Parenthood what it had asked for.

A somewhat more complex problem might arise. What if a member agency otherwise worthy of support should threaten secession if its requests for support are not met? Receiving United Way support in effect imposes some moral constraints on member agencies, and these constraints would be violated if an agency were to demand a dollar amount or a percentage of the nondesignated allocation. In that case, the United Way board would have to take a firm stance with the agency if the United Way system is to be preserved; the issues concern the needs of the less visible or powerful agencies and the board's role as a guarantor and honest broker. Capitulation would essentially reduce United Way to a fund-raising organization.

Conclusion

The process of specifying identity, of being a responsible community of interpretation sensitive to fiduciary duties, changing needs, and the common morality, is painful and filled with ambivalence and ambiguity. In the case just discussed, for example, Planned Parenthood supporters thought United Way did the right thing—supporting Planned Parenthood—for the wrong reason—pragmatics rather than principle; from the point of view of Right to Life, United Way caved in.

Similarly, no general public agreement emerged regarding the actions taken at the Corcoran or at the University of Chicago Hospital. In all of these cases, we see the importance of board self-consciousness about the organization's niche or role in the overall provision of human services. It becomes clear that it is essential to have developed a habit of discussion of issues at the core of the institution's life, of learning about and educating the larger community of which the organization is a part. Specification of mission occurs in a context; it may involve controversy; and it cannot be done well unless the community of interpretation is functioning.

Sometimes, however, a conflict may be more intrinsic to the life of an institution. I turn to that sort of situation in the next chapter.

5

CONFLICTING BASIC DUTIES

TRUSTEES MAY BE confronted with deeply conflicting duties. Contradictions at the core of their organization's mission may become obvious only in particular times and places; they may arise as trustees reinterpret institutional mission to forge a new identity; they may reveal deep conflicts between the vision of the world at the heart of the organization and that of the larger society. On the whole, I will argue for a strategy of accommodation and compromise within some specific parameters.

It will be most helpful to begin with a situation in which the conflict was agonizing, a situation in which the sponsor's vision and identity conflicted with the identity of the sponsored activity. In this kind of conflict, a board's resources and integrity are tested most severely. Other governance mechanisms can handle everything else, including financial integrity. But an institutional identity crisis demands a board habituated to reflection and accountability. It is very easy for the board to surrender to one or another of the conflicting purposes; it is also easy to duck the issues. Trusteeship requires finding a compromise that can be embraced with integrity.

Catholic University of America and Charles Curran

Finding its own proper vocation can be a serious challenge for a board, but the task can be greatly complicated in a climate of legitimate uncertainty about the objectives of the organization, or if the organization has two objectives that push in conflicting directions. Some of the old moralists called the first of these issues the problem of *doubt*; it occurred when clear guidance or precedents were lacking. The second they called the problem of *perplexity*, in this technical sense, an individual or group is perplexed when clearly relevant precedents or principles exist but they pull in opposite directions. A structured moral dilemma exists.[1]

Viewed in its best light, the situation at SMU that I discussed in chapter 3 was one of doubt—doubt about the right policy toward support of athletics, doubt about what steps should be taken to extricate the university from a bad situation. No one could seriously argue that athletics ought to be more important than the academic mission of the university. In contrast, the board at Catholic University of America (CUA) was perplexed, torn between two foundational and, in themselves, compelling claims.

Charles Curran is an extremely well-known Roman Catholic moral theologian who began teaching at CUA in 1965. During the late 1960s, Curran's comparatively liberal views on sexual ethics became a major focus of controversy at CUA and indeed in American Roman Catholicism. (He opposes universal bans on artificial contraception, on masturbation, and on homosexual acts.) The issue first arose in 1967 when the CUA trustees voted not to renew his contract; the theology faculty rallied behind Curran, a strike was called, and the university was effectively shut down. Some members of the College of Cardinals rose to Curran's defense. The trustees changed their minds and offered him a new contract with promotion. A year later, Curran rejected portions of *Humanae Vitae*, the papal encyclical on birth control;[2] his stance led to a second unsuccessful attempt to remove him from the faculty.

Partly in response to these events, CUA reformed its policies to clarify and reaffirm its identity as an American research university; still, it had been chartered by the Pope in the last century, maintained ecclesiastical faculties, and continued the tradition of having American members of the College of Cardinals serve on its board of trustees. In fact, the university's bylaws stipulate that the forty-member elected board should be composed of twenty lay and twenty clerical representatives, and that sixteen of the twenty clergy must be members of the National Conference of Catholic Bishops.[3] Of special relevance is the fact that members of the ecclesiastical faculties must have a "canonical mission" from the ex officio chancellor of the university, who is the Archbishop of Washington, D.C.

In effect, the canonical mission is a license that certifies that the faculty member can "teach in the name of the Church."[4]

A popular teacher and prolific author, Curran was rapidly promoted and by 1971 was tenured, but controversies over his opinions on some church teachings continued. His high profile made him a natural target for those whose theology, ethics, or views on moral questions were more conservative. The Vatican officials responsible for oversight of doctrinal orthodoxy, the Sacred Congregation for the Doctrine of the Faith,[5] opened a dossier on his work, and speculation continued for decades within Catholicism and among observers of the Catholic scene about whether, when, or how he would be disciplined.

The Sacred Congregation finally announced the conclusions of its investigation of Curran in the summer of 1986. Nine months earlier, its head, Joseph Cardinal Ratzinger, had informed Curran of its conclusions and urged him to reconsider his views. While on a trip to Rome, James Cardinal Hickey, Archbishop of Washington and ex officio chancellor of CUA, attempted a reconciliation; Curran later flew to Rome to attempt to work out "a compromise whereby he [Curran] would continue to teach moral theology but not in the field of sexual ethics."[6] The compromise was rejected; in July 1986 Ratzinger wrote to Curran: "[T]he authorities of the Church cannot allow the present situation to continue in which the inherent contradiction is prolonged that one who is to teach in the name of the Church in fact denies her teaching."[7]

The letter was sent to Hickey, who held it for three weeks while Curran was on vacation. Hickey and CUA's board had some difficult choices to make. The core issue was simple enough. As devout members of the Roman Catholic Church, they were bound by its processes and procedures; those procedures had clearly produced a verdict. But the board was also responsible for the identity of an American university, and American universities have historic and plausible commitments to academic freedom. Which master did they serve?

In the event, when Chancellor Hickey presented this letter to Curran he offered his own conclusion that the Sacred Congregation's statement—which had been approved by the Pope—was "incontrovertible proof that you can no longer exercise the function of a Professor of Catholic Theology" at CUA. He informed Curran that he was "initiating the withdrawal" of Curran's canonical mission.[8] The chancellor suspended Curran, and the president canceled his courses.

At this point, CUA's Academic Senate and, more importantly for our purposes, the board entered the fray. An ad hoc committee of the Academic Senate held hearings on the case. They concluded that the chancellor was wrong to determine that Cardinal Ratzinger's letter from Rome was "directly and immediately controlling";[9] for them, the question of church authority was more complex. They thought arguments against the Sacred Congregation might be advanced in good faith, and that withdrawal of the canonical mission would compromise both Curran's tenure and CUA's academic mission. They recommended a compromise in which Curran's canonical mission could be withdrawn if he were to remain able to teach theology, ideally in the ecclesiastical School of Theology.[10]

Informed by this committee's report, the chancellor and the president and—after hearing presentations from Curran and his attorney—the board accepted the senate committee's compromise recommendation in part. They decided that Curran's canonical mission should be immediately withdrawn, but they instructed the president to find an alternative teaching slot for Curran "within an area of his professional competence."[11] The senate committee strongly endorsed the idea of finding a spot outside the ecclesiastical faculties for Curran, but the committee did not want the canonical mission withdrawn until that alternative spot had been found. The committee chair argued

> that the statement of Cardinal Ratzinger . . . is not controlling with respect to Professor Curran's ability to teach in any department outside an Ecclesiastical Faculty. In such departments the University must be guided by the American norms of academic freedom and tenure.[12]

Attempts to work out this compromise failed. Curran's competence clearly was in theology, even if his courses were listed under some other rubric. Curran could not pretend that he was not a theologian, and the CUA administration found the device of a self-proclaimed theologian outside the ecclesiastical faculties to be unacceptable. Curran resigned; he has subsequently held several major academic appointments.

The fundamental conflict raised by this history is reflected in the fact that two responsible and serious studies reach opposite conclusions. The American Association of University Professors, on whose thorough report I have relied, concluded that CUA had in effect "deprived [Curran] . . . of his tenure without due process . . . violated Professor Curran's academic freedom" and that the board, in particular, had failed "to exercise their responsibility to protect the university's autonomy and the academic freedom of the faculty."[13]

In contrast, the judge who wrote the decision in the civil suit brought by Professor Curran found in favor of the university's position. He defined the issue not as one individual's academic freedom, but rather as the freedom of an institution to define its own identity. A faculty contract is set in terms of reasonableness, Judge Weisberg argued, and Professor Curran "could not reasonably have expected that the University would defy a definitive judgment of the Holy See that he was 'unsuitable' and 'ineligible' to teach Catholic Theology."[14] CUA, the judge continued, was "bound" to "accept the declaration" of the Vatican "as a matter of religious conviction and pursuant to its long-standing, unique and freely chosen special relationship with the Holy See."[15] It "could not have given up its right to accept and act upon definitive judgments of the Holy See in its dealings with Professor Curran unless it did so explicitly, which it certainly did not do."[16] The court found for the university, against Curran.

Fidelity vs. the Common Good

My way of sorting out this conflict is to say that the CUA board was caught between the demands of the fiduciary principle, which push it to accept direction from the Vatican, and those of the common good, which entail some agreements about the goods sought by and the demands of justice in higher education. CUA has an identity as a part of the Roman Catholic Church, and it also has an identity within American higher education. The sometimes uneasy relationship between these two ways of understanding itself made the board's task of acting as an interpretative community particularly difficult.

The arguments in favor of the fiduciary principle are particularly strong in this case. If religiously related higher education is to have any integrity at all, the board must have the liberty to define the institution's identity, which means establishing criteria for eligibility to serve on its faculty. A Jewish, Protestant, or Muslim school, as well as a Catholic one, must be able to define the context in which instruction will be conducted. The fact that some members of the faculty, others in the religious community, or the general public, do not agree with those terms—or do not share the school's particular vision of the proper content and function of higher education— could override the fiduciary principle only if the particular college or university were the only source of the goods that higher education can provide.

That is not the case at CUA. Despite its special relationship to the Holy See, its degrees do not open even Roman Catholic doors that cannot be entered some other way. Many other colleges and universities, including Catholic ones, exist in Washington, D.C., and the general area. These considerations suggest the difficulty of denying the university's right to make up its own mind on the issue; it has rights of religious liberty.

On the other hand, identifying oneself with the common purpose of higher education comes at a price. The Catholic University of America is an American university, entitled to the recognition, privileges, and resources of the sort accorded to other American universities, including public financial resources. In *Tilton v. Richardson*,[17] the United States Supreme Court sanctioned federal assistance to Catholic colleges on the grounds that they, in contrast to Catholic elementary and secondary schools, respected academic freedom and were not designed for purposes of indoctrination. Were the Curran case to lead the court to conclude that this distinction is one without a difference, all federal funding for Catholic higher education might be jeopardized.

CUA, with its pontifical charter and historically special relationship to the Vatican, might seem to be an exceptional case which raises unique problems. That is true to an extent, but Canon 812 in the 1983 revision of the Code of Canon Law gives local bishops authority over appointment of theologians to faculties in their dioceses. Should this authority be exercised, as it has *not* been in the Curran case, the problem of nonacademic control over faculty appointments would recur throughout American Catholic higher education. The very passage of the canon (over the objections of leaders of American Catholic higher education) creates a serious problem.

In principle, this conflict between religious purpose and academic self-understanding or autonomy could be disastrous for American higher education. The issues are clearest for sponsored (usually religiously sponsored) higher education. The right of groups to sponsor colleges and universities, and to shape their lives and mission to particular ends, has been asserted since colonial times and, as we saw, was established in the nineteenth century by the Dartmouth College case. On the other hand, members of an academic community may learn that ideas of the sponsor are wrong, imprecise, misleading, or destructive of character. The college's essential commitment to understanding means that those ideas must be discussed inside and outside the classroom.

Thus we have a first-level issue: How can the maintenance of a distinctive institutional identity be reconciled with the demands of a more broadly held value such as academic freedom?[18] This question may well turn into a second-level issue: a debate over the requirements of institutional identity. What does being a Catholic—or Jewish, or Presbyterian—university require?[19]

As they negotiate compromises at the first level, trustees must realize that the demands of both fidelity and the common good—in this case, freedom of academic inquiry—are legitimate. Sponsorship of an academic institution entails giving up something, namely the right to act in ways contradictory to the institution's identity as an institution of higher education. If the sponsor means to maintain an American college or university, it must recognize the rules of the game in which it has chosen to play. The owner of a baseball team cannot unilaterally declare that for his players four strikes are required for a strikeout. Sponsored higher education cannot both claim the rights and privileges the community offers to an academic institution because of its commitment to certain values and violate the community's accepted standards derived from those values. Rights entail responsibilities.

That does not mean that sponsored higher education cannot maintain a vital religious affiliation through elective course offerings, opportunities for religious worship, and sustenance of a campus culture with a distinctive identity. It may even use religious affiliation or religious views as criteria in making some appointments. At this point, the requirements of faithful representation of the tradition or sponsor are likely to come up. No one disputed that Curran taught Catholic moral theology; there were harder questions. Did he in some way distort the tradition? Could he legitimately claim that the views he defended were Catholic views? What, in fact, are the requirements of the fidelity principle?

Catholicism has a distinctive, comparatively clear mechanism and set of procedures for settling these issues. Part of Curran's strategy was to insist that the real issue was the adequacy of those procedures, i.e., to deny that judgments of the Sacred Congregation were controlling for Catholic consciences or institutions. (In religious communities with less formalized procedures, the distinction between procedural and substantive issues may be less clear.) I will say more about the procedural debate in the next section. Whatever the procedures, however, the possibility of conflict between the commitments of an institution and those of the larger society in which it operates remains.

A sponsored college or university confronts important constraints on its actions when it confronts one of those conflicts. It should not pretend to be something that it is not. It cannot advertise a position as if orthodoxy were irrelevant to an appointment when it is in fact central. It cannot constrain the honesty or quest for understanding of its students and faculty. If it takes such actions, it can no longer claim to be an American institution of higher education entitled to the benefits and privileges that college or university status entails.

These ideas can be generalized. If the rationale for trusteeship I have offered means anything at all, it means that the trustees of a private sector institution may take a stand in a social controversy and let that stance determine institutional policy. The hard question is what limits, if any, should be imposed on this organizational freedom.

Consider two very different examples in which freedom might be limited:

1. an organization dedicated to causes the reader must regard as unjust, such as mandatory infanticide of all impaired newborns or legally mandated racial segregation;
2. an organization with a particular religious or other history and identity, which de facto, and perhaps despite its endeavors, finds that a diverse group of citizens depends on it to provide some essential social good such as education or health care.

In such organizations, how much latitude should the trustees have?

In assessing the first type of organization, we must distinguish advocacy from action. Infanticide and racial segregation are issues on which our society has come to moral closure, and our consensus is reflected in our laws. Thus, our commitment to pluralism does not mean that trustees of an organization favoring legal segregation may themselves run a segregated institution.[20] On these issues, as on the importance of freedom of inquiry within the university, we have drawn a line; we have concluded that entrusting people with resources to act on those interdicted ends would be wrong.

On the other hand, we allow *advocacy* of illegal purposes. Because, on my terms, the fact of pluralism strengthens the argument for trusteeship in the nonprofit sector, it would be inconsistent to oppose the freedom of a nonprofit organization governed by trustees to advocate causes, however repugnant the common morality may find them.

We face a somewhat different situation in Case 2 (the dominant organization). Here the issue can arise even if the most fundamental requirements of justice are not violated; at stake may be two acceptable but radically conflicting visions of the good. The question is, "Whose values?" Case 2 raises the issue of paternalism that is always in the background with trustee governance. Should trustees be guided by fidelity to mission or act according to standards supported by their beneficiaries? Their options seem to be betrayal or disrespect.

My suggestion about these difficult situations is that trustees should begin with their understanding of the fiduciary principle and then ask about the justifiability of its implications in terms of values shared with the wider community. It is essential to distinguish among purposes that can be justified more or less well. For example, a religiously sponsored college or hospital must take seriously the mission of its sponsor, but it is also a *hospital* or *college* with a broader dependent clientele that properly expects it to provide health care or educational services. Persons who depend on these services have no right to ask the organization to betray its purposes or surrender its principles. However, insofar as the larger community depends on it for provision of services, the organization must make the case for its controversial policies in the public forum. A policy that departs from a common moral consensus is justified to the extent that case is plausible.

I have tried to illustrate the implications of this idea for the CUA board. To take another example, albeit too briefly for the stakes involved, consider a religiously sponsored hospital in which the sponsor's values impose some restrictions on the medical procedures that can be performed. A clear case is abortion, which is ruled out not only by Roman Catholic theology but by the convictions of Orthodox Judaism as well as those of some Protestant groups. In this situation, the institution faces an obvious and serious problem of hypocrisy if its practices are not coherent with its professed mission.

My inference is that the sponsored hospital's distinctive mission or vocation should limit the services it provides, *so long as they are not generally perceived to be health care necessities.* If services are perceived to be necessities, then the hospital must provide them or give up the social privileges that come with being denominated a hospital (tax exemption, receipt of public funds in payment, etc.). I define a necessity as something for which a generally persuasive public argument can be made. Thus, a hospital that hopes to receive public funds in the United States today must perform hysterectomies, tubal ligations, and autopsies, because there is agreement in the common morality about the fact that those services are medical necessities. But it need not perform abortions, because the morality of abortion is seriously contested terrain in our society.

Obviously, this formula is not a magical device for resolving conflict. It is a rejection of extremes and a call to conversation. Distinctive institutional identity and the fiduciary principle must be allowed some social space, but the standards of the society impose limits. As the Curran case shows, identifying those limits is a complex business that places great demands on a community. I now turn to those issues of process.

Community of Interpretation

I have argued that one primary reason for having a board of trustees is the need to maintain a group of persons who are responsible for ongoing conversation about the hard issues of institutional identity. I also argued (in chapter 2) that board discussions should be open and that boards are well advised to share authority. The board must establish internal and external legitimacy; in the case of CUA that means it must be in real community with administration, students, faculty, and the American Catholic community. In contrast with the SMU board, the CUA board seems to have maintained a good relationship with the administration, but what about faculty and students? The results of negotiations with the Academic Senate are not encouraging on that score.

At least as much to the point is the board's relationship to the wider Catholic community in the United States. Let's assume for purposes of argument that this question is strictly limited to CUA's *religious* identity—bracketing for a moment the *academic* identity issues. On this question, the board's public statements simply announce the conclusion that the Sacred Congregation's judgment settles the issue. But the conclusion is in no way obvious. The exact scope and extent of the power of the Holy See has been the major subject of contention within Roman Catholicism since the second Vatican Council of the mid-1960s. The notion that a papal fiat can legitimately compel all kinds of behavior by people all over the world is a figment of the non-Catholic imagination. On a daily basis, bishops, parishes, and schools have been coming to terms with the issue of authority for at least twenty-five years. They have worked out solutions that range from strict conformity with official teaching through benign neglect to open disagreement. One cannot simply wave a papal charter and dismiss this issue. CUA's trustees were forced to take a stand on the most fundamental issue in contemporary Catholicism: the locus and scope of authority in the Church.

In an interesting discussion occasioned by the Curran case, Joseph Komonchak observed that authority is power made legitimate by the "capacity" to give reasons bearing on a group's common purposes. Actual reasons need not always be forthcoming, but authority, he suggests, is trustworthiness that rests on a habit or history of producing credible reasons.[21] The church, Komonchak concedes, must claim teaching authority because "[i]ntegrity of faith is to the church what territorial integrity is to a nation,"[22] but church teaching is not exempt from the "logic of authority," i.e., the requirement of reasonableness or reference to a "set of meanings, truths and values which define the particular social body within which authority is functioning."[23]

The trustees in fact took a clear stance on the authority question. As Judge Weisberg pointed out, there is nothing surprising or unpredictable about the way the CUA board decided or about the substance of its decision.[24] Professor Curran's "evidence describes the University he wanted to work for, maybe even the one he thought he was working for, but not the one with which he contracted."[25] The board's sense of its own identity and purpose was clearly expressed. It spoke consistently with one important—perhaps the most important—voice in the chorus that makes up Catholic identity, and in particular the identity of CUA.

Those standards may be adequate legally, but they are inadequate morally. To be a true community of interpretation, the board was obligated to give reasons for its actions that were credible to the Catholic community. It had to confront the issue of what it means to be a faithfully Catholic university. The alternative is what I have called trustee fundamentalism: failure to see that an important ongoing task of the trustees is interpreting the meaning of the founding documents and purpose in the present.

The CUA board must maintain itself as a community of reasonableness with reference to shared meanings in at least three constituencies: the CUA faculty and students, the wider Catholic community, and American higher education. If the board's legal authority is to be seen as morally legitimate in those contexts, it must appeal to meanings and values shared within those communities. The contexts are diverse, and disagreements can be assumed. The CUA board members could not find, and need not have tried to find, a position that would please everyone. But they needed to work at understanding and taking seriously these constituencies, and the process should have been open enough to reveal real reasoning and argument. About the only thing that everyone is certain to perceive as *un*reasonable is an unexplained act of—or deference to—power.

I do not mean to argue that CUA's board should have *ignored* the papal charter or the judgments of the Sacred Congregation; they are certainly pertinent. I mean only to say that if they are treated simply as controlling, then the sphere of judgment, or the capacity to interpret, has been removed from the trustees, who ultimately become irrelevant. In fact, in the 1968 debate over *Humanae Vitae* the board appeared to assume more responsibility, accepting in toto a recommendation of a faculty committee that challenged the Vatican.[26] Whatever the reasons, the appearance, if not the reality, was different in the 1980s. If the board is unwilling to take responsibility for independent judgment, it becomes a facade behind which the real power operates. In that sense, the situation is not all that different from what happened to the board at SMU.

Perhaps the CUA board discussed the issue of authority, resolved the issue to its own satisfaction, and then presented a united front to the public. If so, that was a procedural decision of great importance, for it offered the *appearance* of thoughtless obedience to a controversial conclusion. Perceived injustice may be worse if it is seen as delivered without accountability. A hard call is easier to accept if it is clear that all options have been considered.

So long as a pluralistic society carries pluralism to the point that it allows sponsored higher education, problems like the Curran case will recur. Indeed, they are not unique to Catholicism. They can be avoided by eliminating sponsorship or, alternatively, by simplifying governance so that the college is directly controlled by the sponsor—as was characteristic of American Catholic higher education in the first part of this century. That "solution," however, would remove one key unit for reconciling the conflict—the trustees—from the scene.

One important contribution of a board as a community of interpretation is that it is a forum in which *conflicting* purposes can responsibly be discussed. To serve as such a forum, however, the trustees must be able to take responsibility, offering plausible reasons and explanations for their decisions. Trusteeship is constituted by fiduciary duty to a founder, a purpose, or, as in this case, a sponsor, but it is incompatible with mindless deference. The CUA board could legitimately choose to agree with Rome, but the fact that it is a board meant that it had to assume responsibility for that decision.

In fact, a compromise reconciliation may have been possible at CUA. William E. May has suggested a distinction between theological and pastoral authority, arguing that Curran and other theologians rightly claim theological expertise and a related academic freedom, but that "theologians are not pastors in the church." Therefore, theologians are not free to present their arguments and conclusions as if they have been formally accepted by the community as a whole.[27] Dissent must be labeled for what it is. Curran's vision of the church was broader, one in which his views were one of several acceptable options. And he surely would have felt that confining his views to the realm of academic debate violated his academic freedom. I don't want to take time fully to assess the proposal. I mean only to assert that this strategy is the kind that should have been discussed by the CUA board.—And perhaps it was; if so, American higher education and American Catholicism needed to know that the board discussed it.

Conclusion

Trusteeship stands in an ambiguous relation to a pluralistic society. On the one hand, the fact of pluralism argues for the necessity of institutions with diverse moral identities in which governing authority is in the hands of trustees. On the other hand, the fact of pluralism can present problems for organizations with a strong identity, whose vision of the good may conflict with that of the larger society. We should not be surprised by disagreement about the proper resolution of these conflicts. Boards must get into the habit of working them through in a credible way. This assertion raises issues that I will explore in the last part of this book.

PART III

Duty and Character

6

PROCESSES AND PROCEDURES

I HAVE TRIED TO illustrate several different kinds of problems that arise as trustees debate institutional mission. Now we can fruitfully return to some of the general duties of trustees that I mentioned in the first chapter. The first of these duties is good faith support, particularly for the CEO. In a way, this entire book has been about the requirements of support, but I need to make a couple of comments about the trustees' relationship with the CEO in particular.

Two other general duties suggested in chapter 1 are worth stressing. One is a requirement of just or fair dealing. It is important for the board to ensure that the organization not only serves its clientele justly, but that it treats its members justly. The second duty is a requirement of perspective. Boards should retain their preoccupation with purpose and mission and should avoid confusing the fate of the organization with the main thing: the cause for which the organization lives. I will illustrate these last points with two examples from the health care industry.

Good Faith Support for the CEO

It is a cliché of the literature on boards that the most important thing a board does is to hire a chief executive officer. I agree with that cliché in large part. The CEO is the board's chief agent, the person to whom both the organization and the board rightly look for initiation of activity and ideas. Ongoing evaluation of the CEO is an important board activity (as is board self-evaluation). But these important moments of evaluation normally belong in the background. The proper general relationship is one of collegial support.

By collegial support I mean a relationship in which the CEO can count on the good faith and support of the board as well as vigorous and informed discussion and disagreement. My idea of a collegial group is *not* one in which everyone agrees, either because they have been chosen for like-mindedness, or because they are ill-informed—or even because they want to get the meeting over with. By collegiality I mean that the board's members begin with their fiduciary duty to the organization, recognize all actual or possible conflicts of interest, and then contribute their best ideas. They must also have some sensitivity to issues of group process and a recognition that their own views will inevitably have to be altered or compromised.

The relationship between the board and the top staff member or CEO can go wrong in many ways. For example, a board that is too strong may push a CEO aside, as happened in the troubled times at SMU that I discussed in chapter 3. All sense of collegiality and shared power was lost at SMU. The "leadership" wrested control of the situation from the president, from the boards, and from the faculty representative(s)—all of whom were deceived, manipulated, or ignored. The administration was effectively deprived of its power to appoint persons and establish policies that would ensure that the university's highest priorities were retained. Far from assisting the president, or working collegially with him and the faculty, the leadership undercut them at every turn. It failed to grasp the limits of its competence or its role in a large, complex organization.

On the other hand, the Corcoran Gallery's board let the CEO down by being overly passive. Orr-Cahall apparently went to the board's museum committee before deciding to cancel the Mapplethorpe exhibit and asked for advice about the decision confronting her. The board gave her a vote of confidence for any decision she made. She spoke to the president and a number of board members on several occasions before the cancellation decision was made. It appears that the board completely delegated the decision to Orr-Cahall, offering little if any direction. Indeed, pressure to fire Orr-Cahall after the fact was deflected because of this policy. As one board member said:

> I don't think she should be the one who pays for this, regardless of her abilities as a director. They may have to consider that later, but not now. She asked the president [Jewett] what she should do, he told her to make up her own mind, and she did. You can't fire her for that.[1]

Had the board been a more active conversation partner for Orr-Cahall it would have been more accountable and many mistakes might have been prevented.

Board relations with top staff need to move between the extremes of usurpation of power and default. It is not clear that a single optimal pattern exists beyond the general ingredients of collegiality that I have sketched. What is clear is that the board as a community of interpretation must be working with the CEO in an intellectually honest and vital way.

Justice within the Organization

To illustrate the importance of fair dealing within an organization, I will focus on some problems presented to hospitals by HIV/AIDS. I do not want to cover these issues in detail, only to sketch them in order to point to a general area of appropriate board concern.

Providing care to persons with AIDS or HIV seropositivity exposes health care workers to risks of infection—small risks that vary with role. Caregivers have a moral duty to run those risks, for several reasons: The level of risk is low, and health care providers have received social and economic support in their training, thus incurring obligations of gratitude and reciprocity. Arguments sometimes used to the contrary (e.g., that HIV infection should be seen as just retribution or as the patient's fault) seem morally primitive and impossible to generalize; after all, we do not refuse treatment to drunken drivers after their accidents.[2]

Strong as these obligations are for individual physicians or nurses, they are overwhelming for hospitals. Perhaps the risks of working with AIDS patients can justify an individual's decision to avoid, to drop, or to move a practice, but it is obvious that a hospital cannot adopt such strategies. It must provide care. Patients should receive the same treatment whether they are seropositive for HIV or not. At that point, the issue of fair play arises.

On the one hand, some argue that *patients* should be tested routinely, perhaps clandestinely, to detect HIV seropositivity. The test would simply be another of the blood tests routinely done on all patients. This procedure is seldom openly advocated in the United States, but it is done here and has been defended in the United Kingdom.[3] Clandestine testing presents a number of problems, however. It cannot provide a quick and accurate answer to the question of a patient's seropositivity, and it may lead to a false sense of security. It undermines pressure for universal precautions, a much more reliable form of protection for professionals. Moreover, a policy of routine testing inevitably suggests that those who test positive will receive a lower standard of care. Finally, routine HIV testing is unlike other blood tests, where the rationale is protection for the patient; it is prompted not by concern for the patient but for the benefit of the health care team.

If these arguments are persuasive, they suggest that justice requires some hospital personnel to run some risk of infection with HIV. Personnel have no absolute right of immunity from the risk. Obviously, wise management will accommodate staff fears, feelings, and preferences as much as possible. But the hospital's responsibilities set some demands on what personnel can claim as a matter of individual right.

The same kind of situation, albeit in lower profile, will occur in any organization committed to helping people. Stupid and unmotivated students must be taught; the unlovely are entitled to services. The responsibilities of the organization limit the kinds of claims that justice allows personnel to make against it. Some risks and inconveniences come with the territory.

On the other hand, some persons, concerned about HIV transmission from health care provider to patient, push for testing health care workers for seropositivity. The issue turns on "SIPs" or seriously invasive procedures. Most commentators oppose mandatory testing of persons doing SIPs,[4] but at least one writer favors it,[5] and an important legal case[6] takes a middle ground. The most frequently advanced argument in favor of the practice concerns risks of infection to patients; other arguments concern the dementia that may accompany AIDS and risks to health care professionals as their immune systems are increasingly compromised.

In fact, the risk of transmission from health care workers to patients is lower, much lower, than the reverse. In contrast with drug abuse, the simple fact of HIV seropositivity is not correlated with poor job performance. Dementia could be identified independently of blood testing. Because an interval of several months may intervene between exposure and seroconversion, testing would have to be repeated frequently and expensively. Moreover, once hospitals have the information they have serious problems of confidentiality, and they may have a duty to disclose.[7] Politically, if health care workers are routinely tested, their demands that patients be tested will inevitably increase.

Still, no one can assert that the risk to patients is zero, and there can be no doubt that patients want the information, even if its rational relevance is minimal. The best way out seems to be for professionals who perform SIPs to assume a duty of voluntary testing, informed by guidance from national organizations about which procedures they should avoid if they test positive for HIV.[8]

This strategy differs from mandatory testing by the hospital as a condition of employment. Obviously, many employees may choose not to be tested. If a hospital has good reason to believe that specific caregivers are endangering patients, the issue should be brought to the appropriate disciplinary bodies. Work schedules and assignments can be modified as necessary to protect both professionals and patients.

The employees of a hospital retain rights that must be defended against ill-informed demands from the wider community or even from some health care providers. These rights are not absolute, and the degree of risk is of the greatest relevance. Typhoid Mary would have no moral right to continued employment in a hospital, but persons suspected of being HIV positive or even suffering from AIDS do have such a claim, so long as they are not putting patients at risk.

These issues are difficult. Proposing a workable policy is the task of the hospital administration, but it is essential for the board to insist that the organization live up to and respect standards of justice. The board must enter into the kind of argument I have illustrated here and be satisfied that employees are being treated fairly. Discrimination on grounds irrelevant to job performance is about as clear a case of injustice as we can find.

The principle applies throughout the kinds of diverse organizations for which trustees take responsibility. Trustees must insist both that the organization justly serve its constituency and that it itself be a just community. Of course, good faith disagreements will arise concerning the requirements of justice, as my discussion of HIV issues in health care should illustrate. I do not assume that the right resolution to the question of what is a fair policy is ever obvious, or even that all conscientious board members will share an understanding of justice. I only mean to make the point that questions of the just demands of the public and fair treatment of employees must be high on the board's agenda.

The Organization as Instrument

The board should be committed to the organization it serves, offer collegial support for the CEO, and insist that the organization play fair with the wider community and its own employees. But when all is said and done, its commitment to the organization is not absolute. The board must cultivate a sense of perspective on the enterprise, and that may not be easy to do. To illustrate the issues, I want to use the experience of Hospice of Bloomington. I will be discussing a series of events with which I was personally involved, and the reader should be alert for ways in which my participation may skew the analysis.

Medical care in the last half of this century has been remarkably effective in providing cure for disease, but many physicians, hospitals, and patients have been unwilling to admit that the time comes when the party is over—when surgery, radiation, or pharmacology does not help patients but only makes them uncomfortable. Dissatisfied with the kinds of medical care offered to persons near the end of their lives, Dame Cicely Saunders founded St. Christopher's Hospice in London. The hospice was to be a place in which patients could receive care, company, and support as they died. The core idea of hospice was to provide a haven where patients who chose to do so could substitute high quality palliative care—pain control, help with difficulty in breathing, relief from itching or constipation—for active attempts to prolong life. The premise is acceptance of the reality of death for and by the patient.

In the late 1970s, word of the success of St. Christopher's Hospice had spread to this country. Many Americans concerned with the issue made pilgrimages to Great Britain. Hospices had started in a few locations in the United States. Most people familiar with the concept probably thought of hospices as free-standing institutions, but a few hospitals were designating floors or parts of floors as hospice units.

The move to establish a hospice in Bloomington really began in 1978, when an ad hoc group decided to see what could be done. A series of meetings was convened; the group grew and took on a more formal character. Within a few months a de facto board was established comprising academics, clergy, nurses, physicians, at least one attorney, and other concerned citizens. Within a year or two the organization had received 501(c)(3) tax-exempt status as a nonprofit organization, received a grant of $10,000 from a church, hired a part-time staff member, and begun training a cohort of volunteers to assist homebound terminally ill persons and their families.

The board confronted many specific and difficult issues along the way. More important, a broad philosophical issue divided the board from the beginning—an issue that became more explicit with the passage of time. For some board members, hospice was important as a significant form of care that was an *alternative* to the care provided by establishment and organized medicine. Board members might hold this view for a variety of reasons. Some saw mainline health care in thrall to a hegemonic medical profession; others had a vision of a world nurtured in a new religious philosophy; for still others, the basic issue was one of populist democracy. In any case, the conclusion was the same: To preserve itself as a viable option to the existing alternatives, hospice must maintain its institutional independence.

The other camp on the board comprised persons whose objective was not that of providing an alternative, but that of *reforming* the existing health care system. These persons might have a stake in the institutions already providing health care; they might be incrementalists by temperament; they might hold political or philosophical views that were less egalitarian. In any case, they defined success as convincing the local hospital and medical community to embrace hospice and to make hospice services part of the menu that the current providers offered to clients. For them, institutional independence had no particular intrinsic value.

Predictably, the issue was joined because Hospice faced the problems that confront all small, new organizations: time and money. Private philanthropy would bankroll the endeavor for only a limited time; board members, part-time staff, and volunteers suffered burnout. United Way began to provide support in the mid-'80s, but beginning in 1983 Bloomington Hospital (the community's only hospital) was making overtures to the organization, beginning with an offer of office space. How should Hospice respond to this courtship?

In time, the "reformists" won, partly by outlasting the competition. Affiliation with the hospital was gradual, but once informal negotiations were opened in 1983 the end result was predictable. The hospital provided office space and limited in-kind service during an interim period, although Hospice and its board continued as technically independent entities. But in 1987 the board formally voted the organization out of existence and reconstituted itself as an advisory committee for the hospital's ongoing hospice program. Largely due to the abilities of an executive director hired by Hospice before the merger, the program has flourished and in late 1992 boasted twenty-five full- and part-time staff members who typically provided services to twenty-three patients per day.

It is probably obvious that my sympathies lay with the reformists, who ended up winning this conflict. The board's actions illustrate the kind of commitment to purpose, rather than organizational preservation, that I claim boards should maintain. I thought that the board should do whatever it judged would lead to effective provision of hospice services, and I was extremely skeptical about our ability to create and sustain an independent institution over the long haul. Even if major benefactions had supported such a venture, the result would have been inefficient. Moreover, I felt that local medical practice was not as bad as its critics maintained. Insofar as care for the dying in Bloomington was inadequate, it could be improved with time. However, one cannot improve practices or institutions with which one is not in conversation.

Thus, I thought, and think, that when trustees see that their institution performs its best public service by going out of business they should seek to bring about that result—with a caveat and admission of ambiguity.

First, the caveat: The death of Hospice of Bloomington as an independent entity was easy in one respect: No one lost a job. Indeed, the quality of the small staff when incorporation occurred made the merger particularly easy for the hospital. But that is not the only possible scenario, perhaps not the most common one. Often there will be a paid staff, sometimes a large paid staff. I do not want to deny the board's obligations rooted in just claims and gratitude to staff. "Parachutes" may have to be provided; slots in a new, merged organization may have to be found. Indeed, in an extreme case it may be appropriate for an effective organization to preserve itself in order to take on a new agenda—as the March of Dimes did when it shifted its focus to birth defects.

But these considerations do not defeat the basic point, and they must not be allowed to obscure the trustees' focus on mission and community need. They are arguments that suggest sensitivity about the timing and circumstances of organizational death, not the indefinite prolongation of meaningless life.

Second, this story has an ambiguous moral. Something was lost with the demise of Hospice of Bloomington, and that something was the vision of the wing of the original board that preferred independence. From their point of view, Hospice sold out and, at a minimum, lost a leverage point from which to press a comfortable health care establishment. Thus the suggestion that Hospice became redundant is certainly not a value-neutral claim. It reflects my interpretative perspective.

Just so, organizations like Hospice of Bloomington, organizations entrusted to trustees, are never strictly value neutral. By their very existence they stand for a more or less clear vision of the world and the ways in which the world can be made a better place. Disagreement over this vision was the background issue in the arguments on the board of Hospice. Rightly, the issue was seldom joined on an abstract level, but the board had to work out an interpretation of hospice and its relationship to existing forms of care—an interpretation that reflected larger perspectives on the community and social life.

At a minimum we can say that from its own perspective the board acted rightly when it voted for merger. More generally, I claim that nonprofit boards are unworthy of trust if they are unwilling to contemplate steps like those taken by Hospice of Bloomington. Trustees must preserve the kind of perspective that enables them to see the organization as an instrument, as a means to important ends. This stance is quite compatible with vigorous support for organizations in times of trouble. But if the time comes when the board must choose between mission and the organization, mission should win.

Once it is committed to a focus on mission, a board has other duties. It should play fair with the larger community and with its employees; it should be a collegial supporter of the CEO; and it must retain some perspective on the organization. This relationship is complex, requiring a distinctive type of person to make it work. I will say something about the skills of such people in the next chapter.

THE VIRTUES OF A TRUSTEE

THE WORD *virtue* means characteristic or excellence. Thus important virtues of athletes include strength and speed. I want to conclude by identifying the most important attribute, skill, or virtue that a trustee should possess. If it was not obvious in the first parts of this book, the previous chapter must have made clear the extent to which I see trusteeship as a moral matter. In conclusion I want to strengthen that case, to argue that capacities for moral imagination and reasoning are essential in a trustee, and to offer a few suggestions to individual boards and board members.

The first point to be made is that the activities of organizations in the nonprofit sector, organizations of the sort that trustees govern, are moral matters. By that I mean two things. First, and most obviously, nonprofit organizations can affect persons for good or ill. They can and do help, harm, and default. Thus, their performance is never adequately assessed simply in terms of profit and loss, reputation and public relations. Significant goods bearing on health, education, or culture are at stake. Questions about the importance and distribution of those goods are moral issues that must be confronted by trustees.

Second, the range of trustees' appropriate concern with morality is somewhat more extensive than this uncontroversial point suggests. Beyond the questions of "How well are we providing it?" and "Who has access to it?" lie the questions of what *it* is and whether it is worth providing. If, as I have argued, trustees are fundamental custodians of institutional identity, they must be prepared to think about the moral quality of the services they are offering.

The point is so important that I will illustrate it at a little length;

I am particularly eager to show that the question of the moral character of the services provided arises even in situations and contexts where it may seem that morality is simply a matter of the trustee's individual probity or the need to ensure equal access. Those moral issues are important, but they are not the whole story; trustees must be involved in discussion of the worthiness—or value—of the organization's products or services. That is a matter of moral obligation for the trustee, and it comes up even in large organizations committed to goods that are widely perceived to be of value: hospitals and universities.

The Hospital Ethics Committee

It is convenient to begin with hospitals, institutions central to life in the modern world and to which it is assumed everyone should have access. Hospitals are in the health care business, a business whose goals have been hotly debated. Many issues have been discussed for the past twenty years under the general heading of "biomedical ethics." They tend to cluster at the beginning and the end of life and to include such issues as assisted reproduction, genetic counseling, abortion, decisions about impaired newborns, and care for the dying and the demented. The new powers provided by medical science can be used in many ways, and they inevitably create problems of choice over which people can be expected to continue to disagree.

One of several responses to the controversies brewed by medical advances has been the movement to create hospital ethics committees. According to a survey published in *Trustee*, 11 percent of hospitals had ethics committees in 1982; by 1985, the figure had risen to 18 percent.[1] In 1990, the American Hospital Association (AHA) estimated that 60 percent of hospitals had ethics committees.[2] Any development that proceeds at such a pace obviously reflects some sort of perceived concern. The literature discussing the roles and functions of hospital ethics committees, which has experienced a parallel explosions,[3] reflects considerable disagreement—even among writers who advocate the creation of ethics committees—over exactly what their role should be. Options range from conducting educational programs for hospital administration, staff, and physicians, through establishment of hospital policies, to retrospective case discussion, prospective advising on troublesome cases, and even, perhaps, actual decision-making responsibility.

My own opinion, for which I will not try to argue here, is that an ethics committee can be useful in education, retrospective review, policy formulation, and perhaps, in particularly difficult situations, consultation before a hard decision is made. My present concern is in a sense smaller: Supposing that the hospital will have an ethics committee, what relationship should it have to the board?

An ethics committee that is *un*related to the board would be bizarre, for the board—as I understand it—is responsible for defining institutional identity. A hospital that has (a) a board concerned with the vision and values that determine institutional identity and (b) a free-wheeling committee making decisions that determine that identity de facto is in a kind of corporate schizophrenia. Paul B. Hofmann made the point well:

> Trustees are guardians of the hospital's integrity. They have the obligation, and perhaps the burden, of serving as the organization's conscience. Most trustees do not seek this particular role and may not like to be so designated, but they *are* the moral agents of their institutions. One very tangible way to demonstrate a genuine commitment to this dimension of hospital governance is through the systematic development and monitoring of appropriate policies that reflect an ethical sensitivity to the needs of patients, families, and health care professionals.[4]

Hofmann was not arguing for ethics committees, but he was asserting that "the ultimate responsibility for establishing bioethical policies rests with the board."[5] I mean only to endorse this conviction and draw the inference that boards and ethics committees must have some sort of organic interrelationship.[6]

Reasonable persons will disagree about what form this relationship should take, and the right answer doubtless varies from one institution to another. But some of the issues at stake can be identified. First, so far as I can tell, most ethics committees not only are not committees of the board, they do not even include board members. The absence of board members from these committees says worlds about the way boards are perceived by physicians and hospital staffs, and perhaps—sadly—about the time board members have invested in studying questions of bioethics. I have no interest in arguing for the appointment of uninformed persons to ethics committees, but, given the importance of the issues of biomedical ethics in personal and institutional life, a board that lacks members who are knowledgeable about these issues is sadly deficient. How can the board avoid responsibility for the policies with which these committees are struggling?

Let us suppose, however, that knowledgeable board members can be found who are willing to serve on the ethics committee. Who should sponsor the committee? Several arguments have been advanced in favor of a medical staff committee. This arrangement will be palatable for physicians, and it may serve to ensure confidentiality and to open discussion among physicians. A medical staff committee commands authority. On the other hand, the politics of the hospital are such that a committee perceived as a committee of physicians will lack credibility with patients and other professionals who are skeptical about physicians. That is not a small or marginal group.

What is the alternative? An administrative committee may be perceived as having its own agenda—protection of the hospital from legal liability or controversy.[7] Indeed, those same doubts may arise about a board committee, if the board appears to be concerned only with the hospital's solvency and legal liability. It is clear that conflict of interest on the part of committee members should be minimized, and arguable that a board committee—a committee that is not sponsored by a group dependent on health care or the hospital for its livelihood—has as good a chance of being disinterested as any group that could be identified.

My main concern, however, is not with the sponsorship of the ethics committee but with its level of communication with the board. Good communication is possible even if the committee does not include a board member, provided that the institution maintains its integrity and conducts its business consistently with its professed values. At a minimum, the board needs to be able responsibly to discuss, affirm, or overrule the ethics committee.

Incidentally, the ethics committee is not the only committee of the hospital concerned with issues of ethics. Many hospitals have Institutional Review Boards (IRBs), quality of care or quality assurance committees, utilization review and risk management committees.[8] All of these committees, in different ways, make recommendations and set policies that reflect the hospital's vision and values—its identity—and I could make much the same argument with reference to the importance of their close structural relationships with the board. If board members are not competent to serve on these kinds of committees, then something is wrong with the composition of the board. If board members are competent but will be perceived as hostile outsiders by physicians or staff, that strongly suggests the need for an improved level of conversation between the board and its publics.

In brief: A hospital board that is going to play the identity-shaping role I specify must be able intelligently to discuss no-code policies, provision of fertility services, the definition of death, and research policies—not to mention issues of just access to services. The hospital board must enter into the discussion of biomedical ethics.

Higher Education Is Moral Education

Not only hospitals but colleges and universities are inevitably concerned with moral matters—and not just church-related colleges and universities. I take it to be an uncontroversial assertion that colleges and universities should produce students with increased levels of knowledge or understanding. Society is entitled to expect that college graduates understand the world better than they did before they entered college. I have in mind knowing how things, people, and organizations work, what they believe, how they can be expected to act. Understanding inevitably relates to knowing the past of a thing and to comprehending the forces that make it behave as it does in the present.

Someone may argue that the increase of knowledge—through research and teaching—is the sole function of higher education. Even if that were right, there would still be important moral issues of access to higher education, and fair play within the college or university. But higher education is a moral enterprise on a wholly different level. Because higher education is in the business of increasing understanding, it is inevitably in the business of shaping character. It is impossible really to educate while leaving character unaffected. To make the point, I must explain briefly what I mean by the notion of character. We all know what that word means in ordinary speech. We say of somebody, "He's talented, but he entirely lacks character." Actually, the sentence is a misstatement. What we really mean is that the person does not have a character that we find worthy of respect. We inevitably evaluate character, speaking of good guys and bad guys, saints, heroes, and villains.

The relevant fact about character for my purposes here is that it is inseparable from the way we perceive the world. Consider the extreme cases: a paranoid person who knows that everyone is out to get him, or a religious fanatic who is indifferent to suffering because she is convinced that life on this earth is not significant. In these cases it is obvious that these individuals' understanding of the world is inseparable from the kinds of persons they are. My contention is that this is true for all of us.

Knowledge is not something external to the self; it shapes and forms us. When we teach someone to understand, we are affecting that person's character. The process may not always be obvious, and I do not want to reduce my point to the ludicrous one of suggesting that whether or not students know the calculus or what happened at Hastings in 1066 determines whether or not they are good persons. But it would be a tragic mistake to ignore the effect that knowledge can have on persons, and it is inconceivable that an educational institution is doing its job if the curriculum taught by its faculty has no effect on the way its students perceive the world and therefore on their character. The issue is not whether higher education *will* have such an effect, but whether it is self-conscious about it, and whether it is an effect that works for good or ill.

On these grounds, I contend that all education is inevitably a moral enterprise. Whether colleges and universities want to or not, they are doing moral education. Several objections to this claim come to mind. First, it is said that character is formed much more strongly by home environment, earlier schooling, or membership in a church or other voluntary association. The possible effect of higher education is marginal. I do not necessarily disagree with these claims. Certainly higher education cannot be relied on to convert many late adolescent sinners to sainthood. My response is that marginal changes may nevertheless be meaningful changes. Moreover, the subject matter of higher education—in literature, science, and history, in the professions and in research—is so interwoven with questions of power, justice, and the nature of the good life that it is impossible to expunge the ethical dimension from the discussion.

Second, it may be objected that even if we are doing a minimal level of moral education we should avoid being intentional about it. This objection also makes a profound point. I resist the idea that commitment to moral education means formulating and teaching a moral orthodoxy on the campus. In fact, nothing has more severely set back academic wonder and inquiry about moral matters in the past twenty-five years than pressure for premature closure. A college's distinctive contribution to moral education is in empowering and refining the sensibility that its students bring to the discussion. Thus, the test for a college's success as a moral educator does not lie in the specific policies recommended or defended by students but in their reflective habit of mind in considering alternative policy options.

However, resistance to dogmatism—of an old or new sort—does not mean the college or university has no certain moral commitments. For example, all colleges and universities should support a habit of honesty in their students. Even if honesty were not demanded of all persons, the university must make honesty central to its life. In a way, this conclusion follows from the college's commitment to understanding, for understanding within a community requires honest reporting of data, interpretations, and conclusions. We cannot trust the work of fellow scholars if we cannot presume their honesty. The collective pursuit of knowledge is simply impossible if persons are dishonest.[9] In some senses, dishonesty in a university is like infidelity in marriage—a betrayal of the central commitment of the community—and like counterfeiting money—debasing the exchange by substituting something specious for the real thing.

Thus even higher education—so concerned with technical skills, certification, and complex theories—is inevitably involved in moral discussion. Topics of moral relevance range from the priorities assigned to research and teaching, issues in research integrity, and fair treatment of students and employees through questions of multiculturalism, affirmative action, and the role of intercollegiate athletics. The moral ethos or climate of a college or university is of the greatest relevance to its identity, and it is therefore an appropriate matter for trustee concern. If, for example, students are uninvolved with the life of the mind, superficial in their social and political views, and unwilling seriously to discuss religious and moral matters, that reflects a moral problem with the college or university community.

A good trustee of a college or university must be able intelligently to discuss these moral topics. College and university trustees should inform themselves on issues of higher education in much the same way that hospital trustees should inform themselves on issues of biomedical ethics. In neither case is it enough simply to listen to public complaints, relevant and fair as they may be. The trustee must read, listen, and think through the issues. It is a hard job.

The Moral Virtues of the Trustee

I have tried to show that universities and hospitals, large institutions with well-developed staffs, engaged in meeting needs that everyone acknowledges are real, are deeply involved in moral matters and that those matters must come to the attention of the institutions' trustees. I do not mean in either case to argue that trustees should arrogantly pronounce on such matters; rather, these are matters in which trustees should be interested and about which they should develop expertise that at least parallels their expertise in financial management, public relations, or service delivery.

This fact simply reinforces a thesis running through this book: that the optimal trustee is someone willing and able to discuss and assess the identity of the organization, someone with moral insight, sensitivity, savvy, and the ability to consider options reasonably.

That such a conclusion should come from an author who is himself a professor of ethics is scarcely surprising. I hasten to add, however, that I do not mean to argue for boards composed of professional philosophers or clones of Mother Teresa. To be sure, sainthood and skills in moral argument may well be assets in board members, but saints can be unrealistic, and academic moralists are not always insightful. Boards require realism and insight.

Rather, I urge that boards as communities of interpretation be *communities* in which complementary casts of mind and experience can be found. A good board will include members who come from all walks of life. They must, however, share a common ground: a willingness to work together in establishing the moral identity of the organization for which they have taken responsibility. They must be willing to talk together candidly and to recognize that they must reach closure. A board unwilling to wonder together and unable to join issues at the moral level has no business being entrusted.

Nine Concluding Comments

This book has been long on general discussion and short on specifics. Perhaps that is inevitable from my kind of academic, but I want to conclude with an imagined conversation with the reader who has stuck with me so far. The subjects range from some first thoughts on practical questions to a couple of observations about the context of the entire enterprise.

1. What if our board is completely unlike the ideal "community of interpretation" that you propose? What should we do?

Be patient, handle the practical matters as best you can, and work to improve the board's composition and procedures. Many organizations do very well with a simply ghastly board. Perhaps it is better to have a vacuous board than a bad one, but I believe that a good board can make an invaluable contribution. What constitutes improvement? I define a community of interpretation as a group that can talk together about serious matters of mission, justice, and personnel.

2. Our board is not perceived to be representative. We have lost credibility in the community.

Diversity on the board is important, and new voices must be heard. The board will have nothing to interpret if it does not listen. But it must listen to several voices. If diversity simply leads to persons shouting at each other, the board will accomplish nothing. Think in terms of points of view that must be heard, and of persons who will both effectively express them and listen to others, not in terms of the interest groups that may insist on having spokespersons on the board.

3. You have said very little about money and financial accountability. But those are the things we have come to expect—and that the law demands—from our trustees.

I have nothing against money; I expect trustees to take seriously their responsibilities as fiscal fiduciaries. I do not mean in any way to devalue the contribution some trustees make through their generosity or their business skills. But I strongly believe that the logic of nonprofit life easily traps boards into thinking only about money, or thinking of money outside of the context of mission, justice, and the common good. Participation on a board should be enjoyable, and the core of that enjoyment comes from identification with and a sense of contribution to the cause or causes for which the organization stands. Whatever board members' walks of life, whatever their resources, they must be mentally engaged with the most fundamental issues on the organization's agenda. Any pragmatically justified departures from this norm should be seen as exceptional and temporary.

4. So, the board is to think deep thoughts and let the organization go down the tubes?

It is possible to think deep thoughts without letting the organization go to rack and ruin. I agree that boards should be highly pragmatic in their quest for money, and compromise is not a four-letter word in my moral vocabulary. That said, there is such a thing as betrayal of fundamental principles, and, at another extreme, there are times when an organization has outlived its usefulness. Trustees must be ready to recognize those situations when they appear. That capability is an important corollary of the stress on mission. I should add that "deep thoughts" need not be couched in rarefied terms.

5. My experience as a trustee is sitting through bewildering meetings. Much of our time is spent on financial statements I don't understand. I am befuddled and contribute nothing. It's a waste of time.

You should insist on an improved set of procedures for board meetings. The agenda should be planned so that discussion time focuses on the key conceptual issues facing the board, and the relevant facts should be plainly and simply presented. Ensuring appropriate allocations of time is the responsibility of the board chair and the CEO.

That said, you must learn how to read the organization's financial reports, at least well enough to track long-range trends of relevance to the organization's ability to carry out its mission. *The budget should follow from the mission,* and the two should be correlated.

More than that, however, you should confer widely about the issues your organization confronts. There is nothing wrong with reading a good book on health care, higher education, or the arts, visiting a gallery or museum elsewhere, talking to doctors in other communities, or going to conferences at which the problems of American higher education are discussed. Something is wrong if your work on the board has no relationship with those kinds of activities.

6. I am concerned that our board is too passive. We are said to be in the pocket of an experienced and powerful CEO. We are making unpopular decisions, and people are on our case.

Are the critics right? Is there no serious discussion of options at board meetings? Has the board informed itself? Does the CEO respond to questions? A tough balance must be maintained here. On the one hand, the board should seriously discuss options with the

CEO; it will rely on her or his leadership to focus the issues, and then it owes the CEO candid discussion and feedback. There can be no interpretative community without candor. On the other hand, no organization can survive long if the board and CEO are at loggerheads. A good working relationship will always be open to the charge of cooptation.

Assuming that the charge is not justified on the merits, there are at least two important ways to respond to the charge. First, the board must comprise persons whose independent judgment is respected and who are known to have sufficient experience, credentials, or stature to resist cooptation. Rightly or wrongly, public perception of these qualities is important. It is not enough to be of independent mind; one must be perceived as the kind of person who thinks for oneself.

Second, as I said in the first and fifth chapters, a board must make public its deliberations and struggles with hard issues. Exactly when and how to solicit public input and discussion are difficult questions; boards are not the same thing as politically representative bodies. A board defaults if it settles hard issues by referendum or plebiscite. But it also defaults if it does not listen, or if it stupidly fails to take advantage of experience, expertise, and wisdom in the wider community.

7. I am particularly worried about conflicts of interest. Our organization seems to be run solely for the benefit of its employees. The wider community interest has been forgotten.

If that is true, it is a serious problem that should be of the greatest concern for the trustees. To determine whether it is true, one must evaluate the quality of services the organization provides and the level of access to those services for persons who need them. Is the organization spending too much on plant or personnel *in order to provide this quality and quantity of service?* Is it possible that the quality of service is higher than needed?

As I write, many nonprofit organizations are under great pressure to "function more like a business," to be lean, mean, and competitive. That pressure can be beneficial, but it often translates into a demand that more persons with business experience serve on the nonprofit board. The idea is that they will be intolerant of inefficiency.

Although that orientation may be helpful, it is nevertheless important to see that business, political, or professional members of the board of a local nonprofit may have serious conflicts of interest. A board member who is an administrator of a major local employer, for example, faces a serious dilemma when the hospital board votes on a rate increase. The increase may be necessary to maintain the level of patient services, but the cost will be passed along to the employer in the form of higher health insurance premiums. Physician members of the board face a parallel issue as a hospital contemplates mergers or acquisition of physician practices.

Both of these illustrations may be quickly debated. I certainly do not mean to imply that doctors, lawyers, and merchant chiefs cannot rise above self-interest; they do it all the time. I only mean to suggest that the charge of misplaced priorities can be focused in more than one direction. The way around the problem is relentless focus on pursuit of the organization's mission.

8. You are a professor of religion, but you haven't talked much about the religious roots of trusteeship. Serving as a trustee is something I do because of my own religious loyalties and commitments.

My interpretation of the moral responsibilities of trustees is heavily influenced by the theological work of H. Richard Niebuhr and Dietrich Bonhoeffer. In fact, there are only a few explicit biblical references to trusteeship. The more common term is "stewardship." For example, in Genesis 2, Adam and Eve have responsibilities to the Garden of Eden to "till it and keep it." But beyond these references, the general idea of finding oneself entrusted with responsibility for something on behalf of someone else is arguably the central metaphor for the moral life in Jewish and Christian ethics. Part of what it means to be a Christian or a Jew is to take responsibility for one's actions as a trustee of God's world. One valuable effect of the monotheistic traditions can be to encourage persons to see themselves as trustees of resources they did not create.

9. So, what else haven't you told us?

The relationship between trusteeship and trust is something worth thinking about. A trustee should be trustworthy, indeed should be trusted. If we have serious problems of cynicism and alienation from institutions in America today, it would not hurt for us to have more trustworthy trustees. Trust should not be a matter of blind faith; it inevitably involves a certain amount of risk. We need more trustees who are the sort of people on whom others will make a bet, or take a chance.

I hope I have said enough to focus more attention on the moral responsibilities of trustees. Trusteeship is essential to pluralistic democracy as it has evolved in the United States. We should be engaged in ongoing conversation about its strengths, failures, and possibilities.

NOTES

Preface

1. I take this distinction from Kenneth Kirk, *Conscience and Its Problems: An Introduction to Casuistry* (London: Longman's Green, 1927), pp. 255–56.

1. The Moral Core of Trusteeship

1. See, for example, Walter W. Powell, ed., *The Nonprofit Sector: A Research Handbook* (New Haven: Yale University Press, 1987); Richard P. Chait, ed., *Trustee Responsibility for Academic Affairs* (Washington, D.C.: Association of Governing Boards of Universities and Colleges, 1984); Richard P. Chait, Thomas P. Holland, and Barbara E. Taylor, *The Effective Board of Trustees* (New York: American Council on Education/Macmillan, 1991); Clark Kerr and Marian L. Gade, *The Guardians: Boards of Trustees of American Colleges and Universities—What They Do and How Well They Do It* (Washington, D.C.: Association of Governing Boards of Universities and Colleges, 1989); and Miriam Mason Wood, *Trusteeship in the Private College* (Baltimore: Johns Hopkins University Press, 1985).

2. H. Hansmann, "Economic Theories of Nonprofit Organizations," in W. W. Powell, ed., *The Nonprofit Sector* (New Haven: Yale University Press, 1987), p. 28.

3. Lester M. Salamon, "Partners in the Public Service: The Scope and Theory of Government-Nonprofit Relations," in W. W. Powell, ed., *The Nonprofit Sector* (New Haven: Yale University Press, 1987).

4. Richard Fraher, "The Historical Origins of Trusteeship and Charitable Foundations," unpublished paper presented at Poynter Center seminar on the duties of trustees, Bloomington, Indiana, February 16, 1989.

5. Robert N. Bellah et al., *Habits of the Heart: Individualism and Commitment in American Life* (Berkeley: University of California Press, 1985), pp. 152–53.

6. The John D. and Catherine T. MacArthur Foundation, "Facts about the John D. and Catherine T. MacArthur Foundation," Chicago, n.d.

7. *Dartmouth College v. Woodward*, 4 Wheaton 518 (1819).

8. See Leonard W. Levy, "*Dartmouth College v. Woodward*" in Leonard W. Levy, Kenneth Karst, and Dennis Mahoney, *Encyclopedia of the American Constitution* (New York: Collier Macmillan, 1986), vol. I, pp. 537–39.

9. Andrew A. Lipscomb, ed., *The Writings of Thomas Jefferson*, Monticello Edition (Washington, D.C.: no publisher, 1904), vol. XV, pp. 46–47, as cited in Jurgen Herbst, *From Crisis to Crisis: American College Government 1636–1819* (Cambridge: Harvard University Press, 1982), p. 236.

10. Herbst, *From Crisis to Crisis*, p. 234.

11. Merrimon Cuninggim, *Private Money and Public Service* (New York: Mc-Graw-Hill, 1972), p. 78.

12. Formulation of the distinction is taken from James F. Childress, *Who Should Decide? Paternalism in Health Care* (New York: Oxford University Press, 1982).

13. Cuninggim, *Private Money*, p. 253.

14. Ibid., p. 254.

15. Charles E. Rosenberg, *The Care of Strangers* (New York: Basic Books, 1987), p. 17.

16. Ibid., p. 19.

17. Ibid., p. 24.

18. Ibid., p. 35.

19. Josiah Royce, *The Philosophy of Loyalty*, in John D. McDermott, ed., *The Basic Writings of Josiah Royce*, vol. 2 (Chicago: University of Chicago Press, 1969), pp. 965–69.

20. Eleanor L. Brilliant, *The United Way: Dilemmas of Organized Charity* (New York: Columbia University Press, 1990), p. 18.

21. Ibid., pp. 18–19.

22. See Wood, *Trusteeship in the Private College*, and Chait, ed., *Trustee Responsibility for Academic Affairs*.

23. Melissa Middleton, "Nonprofit Boards of Directors: Beyond the Governance Function," in W. W. Powell, ed., *The Nonprofit Sector* (New Haven: Yale University Press, 1987), p. 143.

24. Hannah Pitkin, *The Concept of Representation* (Berkeley: University of California Press, 1967), p. 129.

25. Niklas Luhmann, *Trust and Power* (New York: John Wiley, 1979, p. 62.

2. Two Major Objections

1. Charles E. Rosenberg, *The Care of Strangers* (New York: Basic Books, 1987), pp. 19–24.

2. Ibid., p. 52.

3. Ibid., pp. 274–76.

4. Willard Gaylin, "New Responsibilities/New Anxieties: The Changing Nature of Being a Hospital Trustee," a speech presented at a conference on "Allocating Limited Healthcare Resources: Balancing Fiscal and Moral Responsibility," sponsored by the Health Trustee Institute, Cleveland, May 2, 1991.

5. Thorstein Veblen, *The Higher Learning in America* [1918], as quoted in Max Lerner, ed., *The Portable Veblen* (New York: Viking, 1950), pp. 510–11.

6. Ibid.

7. David Riesman, "Introduction" to Thorstein Veblen, *The Higher Learning in America* [1918] (Stanford, Calif.: Academic Reprints, 1954), pp. xii–xiii.

8. Ibid., p. xi.

9. Ibid., pp. xii–xiii.

10. If, in fact, knowledge about things academic is especially important in trustees, nothing prevents asking academics currently on other faculties—or emeriti—to serve in the trustee role. Faculty from other institutions may well be distinguished by their ability to have some perspective on faculty-board interaction.

11. Amy Gutmann, *Democratic Education* (Princeton: Princeton University Press, 1987), p. 192.

12. Ibid., p. 191.

13. Kenneth P. Mortimer and T. R. McConnell, *Sharing Authority Effectively* (San Francisco: Jossey-Bass, 1978), pp. 23–24.

14. Richard Chait, "The Role and Responsibility of the Academic Affairs Committee" in Richard Chait, ed., *Trustee Responsibility for Academic Affairs* (Washington, D.C.: Association of Governing Boards, 1984), pp. 8–9.

15. Michael Walzer, *Spheres of Justice* (New York: Basic Books, 1983), p. 87.

16. Ibid., p. 92.

17. Richard Fraher, "The Historical Origins of Trusteeship and Charitable Foundations," unpublished paper presented at Poynter Center seminar on the duties of trustees, Bloomington, Indiana, February 16, 1989.

18. James Douglas, *Why Charity? The Case for a Third Sector* (Beverly Hills, Calif.: Sage, 1983), p. 116.

19. Ibid., p. 117.

20. Burton Weisbrod, "Towards a Theory of the Nonprofit Sector" in Edmund S. Phelps, ed., *Altruism, Morality and Economic Theory* (New York: Russell Sage, 1975).

21. I do not concede that public education must remain neutral on all value questions. Indeed, as this argument develops, it will become clear that the real distinctions between public and private institutions are less easily drawn than is often supposed. For helpful discussions of the rationale for and ambiguities of nonprofit organizations, see James Douglas, *Why Charity?* and "The Political Theory of Non-Profit Organizations," in W. W. Powell, ed., *The Nonprofit Sector* (New Haven: Yale University Press, 1987); and Merrimon Cuninggim, *Private Money and Public Service* (New York: McGraw-Hill, 1972).

22. Walzer, *Spheres of Justice*, p. 92.

3. An Illustration

1. *The Chronicle of Higher Education*, vol. 36, no. 23 (February 21, 1990): 37.

2. *Bylaws of Southern Methodist University* 2.01 (a), 2.05–2.12.

3. *Articles of Incorporation of Southern Methodist University* VI.1.

4. *The Bishops' Committee Report on SMU*: Report to the Board of Trustees of Southern Methodist University from the Special Committee of Bishops of the South Central Jurisdiction of the United Methodist Church, Friday, June 19, 1987 (hereafter *Bishops' Report*), p. 12. My discussion of the SMU case is heavily dependent on this excellent report, the product of a special investigation conducted after the full extent of the scandal was revealed.

5. *Bishops' Report*, p. 16.

6. Ibid. See David Whitford, *A Payroll to Meet* (New York: Macmillan, 1989), pp. 126–27.

7. Quotations attributed to Clements in *Bishops' Report*, p. 18; see Whitford, *Payroll*, pp. 130, 133.

8. Quoted in *Bishops' Report*, p. 20; see Whitford, *Payroll*, p. 138.

9. Whitford, *Payroll*, p. 145.

10. Ibid., pp. 151–53.

11. *Bishops' Report*, p. 15.

12. Ibid., p. 26.

13. Ibid., p. 23.

14. Ibid.

15. Ibid., p. 29.

16. Ibid., p. 35.

17. Ibid., p. 36; and in February to the trustees, ibid., p. 37.

18. Whitford, *Payroll*, pp. 204–205.

19. Ibid., p. 210.

20. *Bishops' Report*, pp. 40–41.

21. Ibid., p. 45.

22. Ibid. The bishops who wrote this report explicitly include themselves in this judgment as trustees. Members of the Board of Trustees may have faced legal liability for failing in a duty of due care. In at least one court case, members of a hospital finance committee were found to have a duty to check on what was going on; the facts that duties were delegated and/or that meeting attendance was perfunctory were not an adequate defense. See *David M. Stern v. Lucy Webb Hayes National Training School for Deaconesses and Missionaries* (the "Sibley Hospital case"), 381 F. Supp. 1003 (1974), especially pp. 1015, 1020.

23. *Bishops' Report*, p. 46.

24. Some justification for this view might be found in the university's mission statement: "In service, the University has as its primary responsibilities instruction and research, but it must also contribute to the wider community. Its endeavors should include service to the local community through continuing education, its museums and libraries, performing arts, public lectures, *athletic events*, consultative services and other outreach activities." *SMU Undergraduate Bulletin*, p. 16. (Emphasis added.)

25. *Bulletin of the Southern Methodist University*, p. 16.

26. *The Book of Discipline of the United Methodist Church 1984* (Nashville, Tenn.: United Methodist Publishing House, 1984).

27. Ibid., para. 1513, p. 538.

28. Ibid., para. 1517, p. 544.

29. Ibid., para. 1519, p. 564.

30. "The Relatedness and Independence of Church Sponsored Higher Education," an address to the Texas United Methodist College Association, Southern Methodist University, February 5, 1985, p. 7.

31. For a discussion of these issues, see Murray Sperber, *College Sports Inc.: The Athletic Department vs. the University* (New York: Holt, 1990).

4. When in Doubt

1. Barbara Gamarekian, "Tragedy of Errors' Engulfs the Corcoran," *New York Times*, September 18, 1989, p. 13.

2. Jo Ann Lewis, "Mr. Levy's Corcoran: The Director and His New Directions," *Washington Post*, April 24, 1992.

3. Jon Van, "U. of C. to Quit Trauma Care System," *Chicago Tribune*, May 1, 1988, p. 1.

4. Katherine Seigenthaler, "Michael Reese Hospital Decides to Remain in Trauma Network," *Chicago Tribune*, March 16, 1989, p. 17.

5. Jean Latz Griffin, "Hospital Network Suffers Blow: Loyola Will Be 3d to Quit City Trauma System," *Chicago Tribune*, September 7, 1989, p. 1.

6. E.g., *Chicago Tribune*, "Chicago's Ailing Trauma Network" (Editorial), November 20, 1988, p. 2.

7. Stanford J. Goldblatt, in "Financial Decision-Making in the Teaching Hospital," interview by Karen Gardner, *Trustee* 42, no. 7 (July 1989): 6.

8. Jeff Lyon, "Liver Surgery Makes History: Transplant from 'Living Donor' Is First in Nation," *Chicago Tribune*, November 28, 1989, p. 1.

9. Stanford Goldblatt, quoted in "Financial Decision-Making in the Teaching Hospital," pp. 6–7, 19.

10. Howard Larkin, "Trauma Center Closings Threaten Other Hospitals," *Journal of the American Hospital Association* 63, no. 4 (February 20, 1989): 22.

11. In Diana Crane, *The Sanctity of Social Life: Physicians' Treatment of Critically Ill Patients* (New York: Russell Sage Foundation, 1975), p. 81.

12. It is not clear what the exact implications of the transplant/trauma trade-off were at UCH. The Division of Financial Management at the National Institutes of Health estimates that NIH spent $187 million to support research on kidney diseases compared to $119 million for research on trauma care in 1992.

13. World Health Organization, *The First Ten Years of the World Health Organization* (Geneva: World Health Organization, 1958). Reprinted in Thomas A. Mappes and Jane S. Zembaty, eds., *Biomedical Ethics*, 2d ed. (New York: McGraw-Hill, 1986), p. 244.

14. Leon Kass, "Regarding the End of Medicine and the Pursuit of Health," in *Towards a More Natural Science* (New York: Basic Books).

15. James Douglas, *Why Charity? The Case for a Third Sector* (Beverly Hills: Sage, 1983).

16. Ibid., p. 130.

17. While it is impossible to obtain accurate figures regarding the number of people who boycotted the United Way drive, negative sentiment can be surmised from the distribution of negative donor designations. Of the 141 donors who made negative designations in 1992, 94 negatively designated Planned Parenthood.

18. It may be relevant to state that the author is also pro-choice. For a statement of my views, see *Health and Medicine in the Anglican Tradition: Conscience, Community, and Compromise* (New York: Crossroad, 1986), chapter 5.

5. Conflicting Basic Duties

1. Cf. Kenneth Kirk, *Conscience and Its Problems: An Introduction to Casuistry* (London: Longman's Green, 1927), pp. 255–56.

2. Curran himself has written extensively about the issues involved. See *Faithful Dissent* (Kansas City, Mo.: Sheed and Ward, 1986), and *Catholic Higher Education, Theology, and Academic Freedom* (Notre Dame: University of Notre Dame Press, 1990). *Faithful Dissent*, written while the controversy was most heated, includes more than 150 pages of documents. *Catholic Higher Education* is a more "academic" statement.

3. "Academic Freedom and Tenure: The Catholic University of America," *Academe*, September–October 1989, p. 27.

4. Ibid.

5. The former "Holy Office," here simply the Sacred Congregation.

6. "Academic Freedom and Tenure," p. 30.

7. Ibid.

8. Ibid.

9. Ibid., p. 32.

10. Ibid., p. 33.

11. Ibid.

12. Quoted in ibid., p. 33.

13. Ibid., p. 38.

14. *The Reverend Charles E. Curran v. The Catholic University of America,* Superior Court of the District of Columbia, Action #1562–87, February 28, 1989, p. 26.

15. Ibid.

16. Ibid.

17. *Tilton et al. v. Richardson, Secretary of Health, Education, and Welfare, et al.,* 403 U.S. 672, 1970.

18. For a discussion of nuanced Catholic—and non-Catholic—suggestions on this issue, see Curran, *Catholic Higher Education,* chapter 3. The issue is in no sense closed. The Vatican has issued an apostolic constitution on the subject (*Ex corde ecclesiae,* August 1990), and a set of Ordinances for the American church is being discussed. See the symposium "*Ex corde ecclesiae* and Its Ordinances: Is This Any Way to Run a University or a Church?" *Commonweal* 120, no. 20 (November 19, 1993): 14–26.

19. I mentioned some Methodist reflections on this issue in chapter 3.

20. See *Bob Jones University v. United States,* 461 U.S. 574 (1982).

21. Joseph Komonchak, "Authority and Magisterium," in William W. May, ed., *Vatican Authority and American Catholic Dissent* (New York: Crossroad, 1987), p. 105.

22. Ibid., p. 109.

23. Ibid., p. 112.

24. *Curran v. Catholic University of America,* p. 26.

25. Ibid., p. 33.

26. See Charles E. Curran, Robert E. Hunt, et al., *Dissent in and for the Church: Theologians and Humanae Vitae* (New York: Sheed and Ward, 1969).
27. William E. May, "Catholic Moral Teaching and the Limits of Dissent," in William W. May, ed., *Vatican Authority*, p. 99.

6. Processes and Procedures

1. Reported in Elizabeth Kastor and Jo Ann Lewis, "Damage Control at the Corcoran: Trustees Panel Will Decide Director's Fate," *Washington Post*, September 26, 1989, p. D1.
2. See David H. Smith, Robin Levin Penslar, and Judith A. Granbois, "AIDS and Aid for Patient and Healer," report commissioned by the Task Force on AIDS Ethical/Legal Working Group, Public Health Service, U.S. Department of Health and Human Services, December 2, 1987.
3. Larry Gostin, "Hospitals, Health Care Professionals, and AIDS: The 'Right to Know' the Health Status of Professionals and Patients," *Maryland Law Review* 48:1 (1989): 12–55. See especially pp. 30–43 and note 114.
4. See Larry Gostin, "Hospitals, Health Care Professionals and AIDS" and "HIV-Infected Physicians and the Practice of Seriously Invasive Procedures," *Hastings Center Report* (January–February 1989), pp. 32–39; Karen H. Rothenberg, "AIDS: Creating a Public Health Policy," *Maryland Law Review* 48 (1989): 93–211; Scott H. Isaacman, "The Other Side of the Coin: HIV-Infected Health Care Workers," *Saint Louis University Public Law Review* 9 (1990): 439–94; Richard G. Vernon, "Employee Testing Raises Workplace Privacy Issues," *Trustee* 40 (June 1987): 19–21; and Ronald Bayer, "The HIV-Infected Clinician: To Exclude or Not to Exclude?" *Trustee* 44 (May 1991): 16–17.
5. Michael L. Closen, "A Call for Mandatory HIV Testing and Restriction of Certain Health Care Professionals," *Saint Louis University Public Law Review* 9 (1990): 421–38.
6. *Leckelt v. Board of Commissioners of Hospital District No. 1*, 714 F. Supp. 1377 (E D La 1989). Cited and helpfully discussed in Gordon G. Keys, "HIV-testing of Dental Students and Faculty: Benefits, Detriments, and Implications," *Medicine and Law* 9 (1990): 918–29.
7. Gostin, "HIV-Infected Physicians and the Practice of Seriously Invasive Procedures," pp. 35–36.
8. Ibid., p. 35.

7. The Virtues of a Trustee

1. Benedict J. Gentile and Marilyn M. Mannisto, "Trustee Survey: Trends in Board Committee Structure," *Trustee* 38, no. 11, (November 1985): 32.
2. Gregory P. Gramelspacher, "Institutional Ethics Committees and Case Consultation: Is There a Role?" *Issues in Law and Medicine* 7, no. 1 (November 1, 1991): 73.
3. See, among others: Judith Wilson Ross et al., *Handbook for Hospital Ethics Committees* (Chicago: American Hospital Publishing, 1986); Ronald E. Cran-

ford and A. Edward Doudera, eds., *Institutional Ethics Committees and Health Care Decision Making* (Ann Arbor: Health Administration Press, 1984); and Mark Siegler, "Ethics Committees: Decisions by Bureaucracy," *Hastings Center Report* 16, no. 3 (June 1986).

4. Paul B. Hofmann, "Upholding Patient Rights through Ethical Policymaking," *Trustee* 38, no. 4 (April 1985): 16.

5. Hofmann, p. 15. Cf. Jim Summers, "Meeting the Hospital's Ethical and Moral Obligations," *Trustee* 40, no. 7 (July 1987): 26; an early call for movement in this direction was Barry S. Bader and Andrew Burness, "Ethics: Boards Address Issues beyond Allocation of Resources," *Trustee* 35, no. 10 (October 1982): 14–20.

6. Cf. Harold F. Olsen, "Hospital Ethics Committees and the Role of the Board," *Trustee* 42, no. 12 (December 1989): 28.

7. Cf. Marilyn M. Mannisto, "Orchestrating an Ethics Committee: Who Should Be On It, Where Does It Best Fit?" *Trustee* 38, no. 4 (April 1985): 17–20. This interesting article is built around short interviews with knowledgeable persons in bioethics (e.g., Ronald Cranford, Alan Fleischman, Frederick Abrams, Norman Fost, Ruth Macklin). Because the quotations have been sorted around a set of themes, however, it is difficult to get a clear picture of any interviewee's complete view.

8. Ross, *Handbook for Hospital Ethics Committees*, pp. 68–70.

9. In this context, I mean to conflate honesty and accuracy, but it is worth noting that they are distinguishable qualities. Scholars (students or professors) are inaccurate if their observations are wrong, if they miscopy, or if their calculations are in error. These are serious failings in scholars, and failings that the college community must take seriously. But they are not the same thing as dishonesty, which amounts to reporting one's conclusions or findings in a partial, distorted, misleading, or deceptive manner. Inaccuracy—at its worst, stupidity—in scholars is a bad thing; misleading or incomplete reports—at its worst, lying—is worse because it is an intentional betrayal of the very fabric of the community.

INDEX

Abortion, 67–72, 83
Aramony, William, 69–70

Bellah, Robert N., 5
Brilliant, Eleanor, 18
Burke, Edmund, 8

Catholic University of America
board of trustees, xi, 75–78; and
the community of interpretation,
84–88; fiduciary principle vs. the
common good, 78–84
Charity Organization Society, 18
Chief executive officer (CEO), 22,
91–93, 111–12
Clements, William, 41–43
Common good principle of trusteeship, 9–15, 49–50; vs. the fiduciary
principle, 9, 16, 78–84
Corcoran Gallery of Art, xi, 53–60,
92–93
Cuninggim, Merrimon, 12
Curran, Charles, 75–78, 81, 85

Dartmouth College v. Woodward, 8–9
Doubt, problem of, x, 74–75
Douglas, James, 36, 67, 70

Education: medical, 62–63; public
vs. private, 36–37, 117n21; religious
and academic, 75–76, 78–82, 84–88
Ethics committees, 102–05

Faculty: and university trustees, 29–
33, 117n10
Fiduciary principle of trusteeship, 5–
9, 45–49; vs. the common good,
9, 16, 78–84
Foundations, 11, 12

Gaylin, Willard, 29
Goldblatt, Stanford, 62
Government: as proper public ser-
vice provider, 33–37
Gurteen, Reverend S. H., 18

Health care, 64–65; government-
provided, 34–35. *See also* Hospitals
Hickey, James Cardinal, 76–77
Hofmann, Paul B., 103
Honesty, 10–11, 107–08, 122n9
Hospice of Bloomington, ix, xi, 96–
100
Hospitals: ethics committees, 102–
05; HIV infection risks in, 93–96;
trustees vs. physicians in, 26–29;
religious, 14, 83–84; voluntary, 12–
14. *See also* University of Chicago
Hospital

Interpretation, community of, ix, 15–
21, 59–60, 84–88, 109–10

Jefferson, Thomas, 9
Justice, xi, 93–96

Kliever, Lonnie D., 42
Komonchak, Joseph, 85

Levy, David, 58

MacArthur, John D., 6
Mapplethorpe, Robert: controversial
exhibit, xi, 53–60, 92–93
March of Dimes, 17
May, William E., 87
Mission, xi, 59–60; conflicts in, 75–
78, 82–84, 87–88; of hospital trus-
tees, 65–66; interpreting, 16–18,

DAVID H. SMITH is Professor of Religious Studies at Indiana University and Director of The Poynter Center for the Study of Ethics and American Institutions. He is a founding member of the Hospice of Bloomington and the Association for Practical and Professional Ethics. His publications include *Health and Medicine in the Anglican Tradition: Conscience, Community, and Compromise.*